Group's®
Blockbuster
MOVIE ILLUSTRATIONS

Bryan Belknap

  LOVELAND, COLORADO

Group's R.E.A.L. Guarantee to you:

Every Group resource incorporates our R.E.A.L. approach to ministry—a unique philosophy that results in long-term retention and life transformation. It's ministry that's:

This is EARL. He's R.E.A.L. mixed up. (Get it?)

Relational
Because student-to-student interaction enhances learning and builds Christian friendships.

Experiential
Because what students experience sticks with them up to 9 times longer than what they simply hear or read.

Applicable
Because the aim of Christian education is to be both hearers and doers of the Word.

Learner-based
Because students learn more and retain it longer when the process is designed according to how they learn best.

Dedication

This book is dedicated to my beautiful bride, Jill, and to my family (Mom, Dad, and Kevin) for putting up with my movie consumption; to Brandon and Mike for joining in my filmmaking; to Bob, Jeffrey, and Group Publishing for encouraging me; to Capra, Hitchcock, Lucas, and Henson for sparking my imagination; and most important, to Jesus for giving me a reason to write in the first place.

Group's BlockBuster Movie Illustrations

Copyright © 2001 Bryan Belknap

Visit our Web site: **www.grouppublishing.com**

Credits
Author: Bryan Belknap
Editor: Kelli B. Trujillo
Creative Development Editor: Jim Kochenburger
Chief Creative Officer: Joani Schultz
Art Director: Jean Bruns
Designer: Ray Tollison
Computer Graphic Artist: Shelly Dillon
Illustrator: Matt Wood
Cover Art Director: Jeff A. Storm
Cover Designer: Wirestone
Production Manager: Dodie Tipton

Library of Congress Cataloging-in-Publication Data
Belknap, Bryan.
   Group's BlockBuster movie illustrations / Bryan Belknap.
     p. cm.
   Includes indexes.
   ISBN 0-7644-2256-1(alk. paper)
    1. Motion pictures in Christian education. 2. Christian education of teenagers. I. Title.
BV1535.4 .B45 2001
268'.67--dc21

                                         00-065462

10 9 8 7   10 09 08 07 06 05 04
Printed in the United States of America.

Contents

Introduction

It's 5:30 p.m. on a Thursday evening. Everything's set—the pizza, the props, the prizes, and the people. You've practiced and polished a talk that will spur your teens to a lifetime of devotion and discipleship to their Lord and Savior. You read your talk one more time and realize...something's missing. You need the spark, the hook that will command attention from the first word and will draw the crowd in for you to lead them toward spiritual truth. You need a sure-fire illustration that will leave them speechless.

They've already heard your personal stories and the ones you claim are true—twice. You dig around the office and the only thing you discover to capture the attention of kids weaned on MTV, X Games, and PlayStation is...a flannel graph.

Needless to say, they laugh at you, not with you.

This example is extreme, but every pastor has moments of desperation—needing an innovative, attention-getting way to start a discussion and ending up with something a little more cutting edge than "Pharaoh, Pharaoh." Worry no more, and get thee to the cinema! *Group's BlockBuster Movie Illustrations* provides a plethora of priceless moments from more than eighty of Hollywood's greatest hits, from classics like *Star Wars* and *Hoosiers* to more recent flicks such as *Galaxy Quest* and *Notting Hill*.

The clips used in *Group's BlockBuster Movie Illustrations* powerfully portray biblical truths in a gripping way that will spice up youth talks, devotions, small-group meetings, retreats, lessons, and even Sunday morning sermons! This easy-to-use collection of illustrations covers more than 160 crucial youth ministry topics, such as dating, materialism, and discovering God's will. And similar to the way Jesus used parables, movies are something we can all relate to—they provide a common point of reference to kick-start discussions that will reach unchurched seekers as well as seasoned Christians.

How to use Group's BlockBuster Movie Illustrations

Do you have a key point or a specific Scripture passage that you'd like to illustrate? Since the clips are organized by topic, simply flip to the themes that tie in with your main point, or select a clip using the Scripture Index. Once you've picked a clip, you'll find that the illustration is divided into several parts. Each movie illustration begins by introducing the theme, title, and rating information of the movie, and includes a Scripture passage that relates to the theme. You'll also discover...

Funny/Dramatic Icons—An icon is shown at the beginning of each clip to let you know if the tone of the movie clip is humorous or dramatic.

HUMOROUS **DRAMATIC**

Alternate Takes—Though the discussion questions focus on a specific theme, each of the clips in this book could be used to spark discussions on a variety of topics. In the Alternate Takes section you'll find other themes and Scriptures that you could use to start a discussion.

Start Time/End Time—These times tell you when to start and stop the tape. Clip locations are determined by setting the tape counter on your VCR to 00:00:00 when the studio logo for the film appears (immediately before the opening credits). All Start/End Times are approximate and are given to closest 15-second interval.

Start Cue/End Cue—If you have an unreliable timer on your VCR, these visual cues specify the action or dialogue that takes place at the beginning and end of each clip.

Duration—Here you get an estimate of the elapsed time of each clip. To keep the focus on the point you want to illustrate and not turn the clip into a full-blown screening, every movie clip is three minutes or less.

Overview—Here you'll get the scoop on the action of the clip and the names of the main characters. To find out more about the plot of the entire movie, check out the details included in the Movie Background Index.

Illustration—What's the point? This is the place to look for a brief explanation of the spiritual significance of the clip and how it relates to teenagers' lives. Feel free to use it as a guide and then explain the main point in your own words.

Questions—Need some discussion-starters? Here you'll find five questions that break the ice, dig into the truth of Scripture, and help kids apply that truth to their lives. Remember, if you're using an Alternate Take, you'll need to come up with your own discussion questions that apply to the theme you've chosen.

After you've previewed the clip and cued the tape to the Start Time, you're ready to dive in! Just make sure you pay attention to a few important details.

Copyright Laws—Believe it or not, the FBI warning at the beginning of most videos is for real! In general, federal copyright laws do not allow you to use videos or DVDs (even ones you own) for any purpose other than home viewing. Though some exceptions allow for the use of short segments of copyrighted material for educational purposes, it's best to be on the safe side. Your church can obtain a license from the Motion Picture Licensing Corporation for a small fee. Just visit www.mplc.com or call 1-800-462-8855 for more information. When using a movie that is not covered by the license, we recommend directly contacting the movie studio to seek permission for use of the clip.

Content—Go ahead and sigh with relief…*Group's BlockBuster Movie Illustrations* contains absolutely no clips from R-rated movies! As you know, even many PG and PG-13 movies contain inappropriate or offensive content. Be sensitive to the fact that some students may view your use of a clip as an endorsement of the entire movie. Do some research! Read the Movie Background Index to find a summary of the plot, and use resources such as the Internet or movie reviews in the newspaper to get a better idea of questionable themes or content. Sometimes it may be necessary to voice a disclaimer, letting students know that, although you value the scene you're showing, you do not approve of the rest of the movie. (For information on illustrations from R-rated films, such as *Braveheart, Schindler's List,* and *The Matrix*, visit Group's Mind Over Media movie clip database at www.youthministry.com.)

I've been very careful to recommend clips that do not have questionable content, though the same guarantee can't be made for the scenes before or after the suggested clip. The most important principle to remember is this: **Preview the clips!** Be careful with VCRs that roll back several seconds when stopped! Make sure you've got the timing just right so that you don't have to spend the next year apologizing for an unfortunate mistake.

Now you're ready to go!

Dim the lights, pass out the ultrafattening popcorn, press "play" on the VCR, and dive deep with your kids into the issues hidden below the surface of the screen. You'll be amazed at the life-changing discussions that will result from even the cheesiest movies, and you'll be thankful that watching movie clips can actually spur your teenagers on to pursue Jesus!

Movie Illustration
THEMES A-C
Abundant Life...The Bible...Covetousness...

★ ★ ★

ABUNDANT LIFE—I'm Sooo Bored!

Title: FERRIS BUELLER'S DAY OFF (PG-13)

Scripture: John 10:10b

Alternate Take: Knowledge (Proverbs 8:10-11)

START TIME: *10 minutes, 45 seconds*
START CUE: *The economics teacher begins his lecture.*
END TIME: *12 minutes, 00 seconds*
END CUE: *The teacher says, "Voodoo economics."*
DURATION: *1 minute, 15 seconds*

Overview: An economics teacher drones on and on while his students exhibit various levels of boredom.

Illustration: Hopefully this scene doesn't remind you of your church service! This memorable scene illustrates many people's perspective on Christian life—it's so boring. Yet the Bible tells us that Christ came not only to free us from sin, but also to give us abundant life in the here and now. Use this clip to start a discussion about how following Jesus should be like going to a party, not like having a root canal.

Questions
- **What types of situations does this clip remind you of? Do you know people who think of church this way?**
- **Why do some people think Christian life is boring?**
- **How can it be exciting?**
  Read John 10:10b.
- **What do you think it means to live life to the fullest?**
- **How can you live an abundant life now?**

ABUNDANT LIFE—Life Is Sweet!

Title: WHAT ABOUT BOB? (PG)

Scripture: James 1:17

Alternate Takes: Hospitality (Romans 12:13),
Thankfulness (1 Thessalonians 5:16-18)

START TIME: *49 minutes, 30 seconds*
START CUE: *Bob and the family eat dinner.*
END TIME: *51 minutes, 30 seconds*
END CUE: *Dr. Marvin says, "Will you stop it?!"*
DURATION: *2 minutes*

Overview: Bob eats dinner and *loves* it, moaning with pleasure the entire time. He continually compliments everyone and everything until Dr. Marvin yells at him to stop it.

Illustration: You've probably displayed such over-the-top appreciation only for your grandmother's fruitcake, but this scene presents a great picture of enjoying life! When God made the world, he said everything in it was good. We do a good job of messing up God's creation, but that doesn't mean God doesn't want us to enjoy what is good. This clip will get students thinking about how to live joyfully and abundantly.

Questions
- **What is your favorite food? Why?**
- **What is your favorite thing to do? Why?**
    Read James 1:17.
- **Does God want you to enjoy life? Why or why not?**
- **What are some gifts he's given you to enjoy?**
- **What can steal joy in your life? How can you begin to enjoy life more?**

ALCOHOL—I Need a Drink

Title: WHO FRAMED ROGER RABBIT? (PG)

Scripture: Ephesians 5:18-20

Alternate Takes: Stress (Philippians 4:6-7),
The Body (1 Corinthians 6:19-20)

START TIME: *23 minutes, 15 seconds*
START CUE: *Roger is distraught over his wife's infidelity.*
END TIME: *24 minutes*
END CUE: *Roger recovers from his drink.*
DURATION: *45 seconds*

Overview: Roger Rabbit takes a drink of alcohol after finding out some distressing news. The liquor turns him into a bouncing, screaming juggernaut.

Illustration: Alcohol abuse changes people, making them say and do things they wouldn't normally do. God forbids drunkenness, and this funny clip should help start a discussion on this serious topic.

Questions
- **Why did Roger want a drink? Why else do you think people drink alcohol?**
- **Does anything good come from being drunk? anything bad?**
- **In what ways do people you know change when they drink alcohol?**
    Read Ephesians 5:18-20.
- **Why do you think God hates drunkenness? How does God want us to live instead?**
- **How can you avoid using alcohol and encourage your friends to do the same?**

ALCOHOL—You Look So Stupid!

Title: THE WEDDING SINGER (PG-13)

Scripture: Proverbs 23:31-35

Alternate Take: Kindness (Genesis 9:20-23)

START TIME: *9 minutes, 45 seconds*
START CUE: *Robbie helps a kid go out the back door.*
END TIME: *10 minutes, 45 seconds*
END CUE: *Robbie says, "I saw a boot come out."*
DURATION: *1 minute*

Overview: Robbie helps a kid who drank too much go outside to throw up. The best man follows, staggering around like an idiot. When the others leave, Robbie and Julia talk about how they don't really like to drink.

Illustration: Drunk people are never as cool as they seem in commercials (probably because drunk people *aren't* cool). This scene illustrates how ridiculous it is to think getting drunk is cool. Robbie helps two drunk people, both of whom look really stupid. Abusing alcohol may seem cool, but it sure makes the drunk person look like an idiot.

Questions
- **What is the dumbest thing you've heard of someone doing while he or she was drunk?**
- **Why do people drink alcohol even though it makes them do stupid things?**
- **When someone gets drunk, what does it communicate to others?**
    Read Proverbs 23:31-35.
- **How can alcohol "bite" you?**
- **How should you deal with alcohol?**

ANGER—How to Lose Friends

Title: WHO FRAMED ROGER RABBIT? (PG)

Scripture: Proverbs 14:17a

Alternate Takes: Dealing With Death (2 Samuel 19:1-4), Righteous Anger (Exodus 32:19-20)

START TIME: *12 minutes, 45 seconds*
START CUE: *Eddie bellys up to the bar.*
END TIME: *13 minutes, 45 seconds*
END CUE: *Eddie leaves the bar.*
DURATION: *1 minute*

Overview: A man taunts Eddie Valiant for his involvement with a "toon" case. Eddie takes out his anger physically on the man because Eddie's brother was killed by a "toon."

Illustration: "Don't make me angry. You wouldn't like me when I'm angry." How many times have you heard that? Today very few people know how to control their anger. In fact, they justify hurting other people because they were once hurt. Thankfully, Jesus didn't share this point of view. We are called to become peacemakers and forgive as Christ forgave.

Questions
- **Was Eddie justified in his actions? Why or why not?**
- **When have you responded in anger to someone? What happened?**
- **How could you have handled your anger differently?**
  Read Proverbs 14:17a.
- **Is anger a sin? Explain.**
- **What are healthy ways for you to deal with anger instead of doing "foolish things"?**

ANGER—I Can't Take It Anymore!

Title: THE WATERBOY (PG-13)

Scripture: Psalm 37:7-9

Alternate Takes: Honoring Parents (Proverbs 30:17), Conflict (Proverbs 15:1-2)

START TIME: *24 minutes, 15 seconds*
START CUE: *The Professor enters the class.*
END TIME: *26 minutes, 15 seconds*
END CUE: *Students pull Bobby off of the Professor.*
DURATION: *2 minutes*

Overview: Bobby answers questions in class with his mother's quaint sayings, not with facts. The Professor tells Bobby his mother is wrong. When the Professor insults Bobby's mother, Bobby tackles him.

Illustration: Do you ever wish you could solve your problems that way? Bobby displays exactly how we should *not* deal with our anger. Too many people go around half-cocked, and they need to take some advice from Jesus and turn the other cheek. Even when something makes your blood boil, you shouldn't release your anger on others.

Questions
- **Has anything ever made you as mad as Bobby was? What was it? Why were you so angry?**
- **What should Bobby have done with his anger?**

- **How do you usually deal with your anger?**
    Read Psalm 37:7-9.
- **Why is it hard to refrain from anger?**
- **How can you apply these verses and deal with your anger in the right way?**

ANGER—Oh Yeah? You're Gonna Get It!

Title: DUMB AND DUMBER (PG-13)

Scripture: Matthew 5:9

Alternate Takes: Conflict (Proverbs 29:8), Revenge (Leviticus 19:18)

START TIME: *1 hour, 17 minutes, 45 seconds*
START CUE: *Mary throws a snowball at Harry.*
END TIME: *1 hour, 18 minutes, 45 seconds*
END CUE: *Harry and Mary laugh at each other.*
DURATION: *1 minute*

Overview: In my humble opinion, this is one of the funniest scenes ever filmed! Mary starts a playful snowball fight with Harry that turns deadly. Harry retaliates like a gladiator, literally pounding her face into the snow.

Illustration: Anger is no laughing matter, but it might take a few minutes for the laughter to die down after this clip. Jesus calls us to be peacemakers, which sounds way out of step with today's culture of protecting "honor" at all costs. We need more peacemakers who turn their backs on anger and keep their fists unclenched.

Questions
- **Have you ever been in a fight? What happened?**
- **Could you have avoided the fight in the first place? How?**
    Read Matthew 5:9.
- **What happens in a fight when someone becomes a peacemaker?**
- **When is it hard to be a peacemaker? Why is it so difficult?**
- **What do you need to change in order to become a peacemaker?**

BEAUTY—As Fleeting As Fads

Title: SILVERADO (PG-13)

Scripture: Psalm 49:13-14

Alternate Takes: Eternal Rewards (1 Timothy 6:17-19), Dating (Proverbs 31:10-31)

START TIME: *50 minutes, 00 seconds*
START CUE: *Paden and Hannah walk on her land.*
END TIME: *51 minutes, 00 seconds*
END CUE: *Paden and Hannah stand in silence.*
DURATION: *1 minute*

Overview: Paden compliments Hannah on her beauty. Hannah says that many men tell her she's beautiful because they are interested only in her exterior. They all leave because she wants to build a life and a farm and a future, not have a temporary fling. She wants to invest her life in something that lasts because she knows her beauty will fade.

Illustration: People typically pursue their "significant others" based on physical attraction, not commitment. (Let's face it, personality and piano skills don't show up in prom pictures!) Yet beauty fades, and it should never be used— by men *or* by women—as a basis for building a future. Use this clip to help your teenagers discover that God is the only firm foundation that stands the test of time.

Questions
- **Have you ever liked someone or dated a person based on his or her looks? What happened?**
- **Why does society place so much emphasis on beauty?**
  Read Psalm 49:13-14.
- **What do these verses have to say about those who build their lives on superficial things?**
- **What things in a person last forever? What should be the basis for romantic relationships?**
- **How will changing your view of beauty help you make better decisions?**

THE BIBLE—Do the Twist

Title: MUPPET TREASURE ISLAND (G)

Scripture: Proverbs 30:5-6

Alternate Takes: Forgiveness (Ephesians 4:31-32), Perseverance (1 Corinthians 16:13)

START TIME: *1 hour, 10 minutes, 15 seconds*
START CUE: *Long John Silver receives the black spot.*
END TIME: *1 hour, 11 minutes, 30 seconds*
END CUE: *The pirates hug Long John Silver.*
DURATION: *1 minute, 15 seconds*

Overview: Long John Silver receives the dreaded black spot—a death warrant. He says he fears for his captors' lives because they wrote it on a page from the Bible. Releasing him is the only way they will escape God's wrath. They do so, thanking Long John Silver for his kindness.

Illustration: Through the centuries, the Bible has been twisted to support almost any cause under the sun. Even today, men armed with a few verses sway people who are not grounded in Scripture to join their heresy. This clip can jump-start a discussion about how God's entire Word is inerrant and must be understood as a whole, not just in bits and pieces.

Questions
- **How did Long John Silver use the Bible to get free?**
- **What are some ways people have used the Bible to support their own ideas and actions?**
- **Why are people sometimes tricked into believing false interpretations of the Bible?**
  Read Proverbs 30:5-6.
- **How do you judge whether someone is using the Bible correctly?**
- **What can you do to gain more knowledge of the Bible?**

THE BIBLE—Reading Under the Lines

Title: WHAT ABOUT BOB? (PG)

Scripture: Revelation 22:18-19

Alternate Takes: Annoying People (Acts 16:16-18), Patience (Colossians 1:9-10)

START TIME: *1 hour, 28 minutes, 15 seconds*
START CUE: *Dr. Marvin starts tying up Bob.*
END TIME: *1 hour, 31 minutes, 15 seconds*
END CUE: *Bob tries to untie himself.*
DURATION: *3 minutes*

Overview: Dr. Marvin ties up Bob in the woods and places a homemade bomb around Bob's neck because he wants Bob to leave him alone. Bob, oblivious to the real danger, interprets the situation as an allegory to his emotional, inner life.

Illustration: Sometimes people pull some pretty wacky personal interpretations out of the Bible! True, it is a living Word that speaks to every person across all time periods, but that doesn't mean everything we interpret it to say is correct. Personal application needs to be mixed with sober biblical scholarship. This silly clip will help kids develop discernment as they approach God's Word.

Questions

- Have you ever known a person who was as out of touch with reality as Bob was in this situation? In what ways did that person misunderstand reality?
- What is the weirdest biblical interpretation you have ever heard?
  Read Revelation 22:18-19.
- Should you personalize Scripture in order to apply it to your life?
- What is the difference between applying Scripture to your personal life and changing Scripture?
- How can you guard against incorrect interpretations of Scripture?

THE BIBLE—Take It to Heart

Title: DAVE (PG-13)

Scripture: Psalm 1:1-3

Alternate Take: The Church (Hebrews 10:23-25)

START TIME: *32 minutes, 00 seconds*
START CUE: *Dave enters the briefing room.*
END TIME: *33 minutes, 45 seconds*
END CUE: *Dave asks if he can keep the pen he found.*
DURATION: *1 minute, 45 seconds*

Overview: Dave enters the room where the White House press conferences are held. He begins to practice giving speeches, reciting verbatim the President's words. Dave talks about the importance of living out the values brought out in the speeches.

Illustration: You can probably recite song lyrics and movie quotes easily ("You talkin' to me?"), but try to recite Scripture, and your brain freezes up! Nothing is more important, though, than having God's Word tucked within your heart. Use this clip to challenge your teens to dig into the Bible. Only when they develop the same passion for learning God's Word as they have for baseball stats or the latest #1 song will they experience awesome spiritual growth.

Questions

- What is something you can recite from memory? Prove it.
- How much Scripture can you quote from memory?
- Is memorizing Scripture easy or hard for you? Why?
  Read Psalm 1:1-3.
- Why is it so important to spend time studying Scripture?
- What are some different methods you might use to help you memorize Scripture more easily?

THE BIBLE—Thee, Those, Thou...Huh?

Title: MONTY PYTHON AND THE HOLY GRAIL (PG)

Scripture: 2 Timothy 3:14-17

Alternate Take: Guidance (Psalm 119:129-133)

START TIME: *1 hour, 12 minutes*
START CUE: *The priests open the sacred text.*
END TIME: *1 hour, 14 minutes*
END CUE: *The priests close the sacred text.*
DURATION: *2 minutes*

Overview: King Arthur gets the holy hand grenade and asks the priest to explain how to use it. The instructions, from a sacred text, are long, drawn out, and difficult to understand.

Illustration: Let's be honest. Some passages of the Bible read like instructions from NASA! Depending on the translation or the passage (Ezekiel, say what?), the Scriptures can sometimes seem inscrutable and archaic to teenage readers. Use this clip to dispel the misconceptions about God's Word and to teach kids exciting ways to study the Bible.

Questions
- **Does the book in the clip remind you of the Bible? How?**
- **What do you find hard to understand about the Bible?**
   Read 2 Timothy 3:14-17.
- **Do you think God intends for the Bible to be difficult? Why or why not?**
- **Why should we study the Bible?**
- **What are some ways to tackle those hard-to-understand parts in the Bible?**

THE BIBLE—What Does It Mean?

Title: THE LITTLE MERMAID (G)

Scripture: Acts 17:10-12

Alternate Takes: False Prophets (1 Timothy 4:1-2), Teaching (James 3:1)

START TIME: *8 minutes, 45 seconds*
START CUE: *Ariel brings what she found to Scuttle.*
END TIME: *10 minutes, 30 seconds*
END CUE: *Ariel swims away.*
DURATION: *1 minute, 45 seconds*

Overview: Ariel shows the "human" objects she found at the bottom of the sea to her friend Scuttle and asks him what they are. Scuttle picks up the objects and tells Ariel the most ridiculous stories about each one's function, filling Ariel with false knowledge.

Illustration: Finding out that a teacher taught you incorrectly is always a shock. When it comes to Scripture, too many people accept everything their pastor says without testing it against Scripture. We must know God's Word so we don't fall for false teachings. Use this clip to encourage your students to be like the Bereans and examine every teaching in order to discover the truth.

Questions
- **What is something you were taught as a kid that you later learned was wrong?**
- **How did that make you feel?**
- **What are some false teachings people have pulled out from the Bible?**
  Read Acts 17:10-12.
- **Why did the Bereans believe Paul's teachings?**
- **How can you be like the Bereans and discern whether people are teaching the truth or not?**

THE BODY—A House Built on Twinkies

Title: GROUNDHOG DAY (PG)

Scripture: 1 Corinthians 3:16-17
Alternate Take: Consequences (Psalm 75:4-7)

START TIME: *35 minutes, 45 seconds*
START CUE: *Phil eats a TON of food.*
END TIME: *37 minutes, 30 seconds*
END CUE: *Phil crams an éclair in his mouth.*
DURATION: *1 minute, 45 seconds*

Overview: Phil consumes more food than the entire offensive line of the Dallas Cowboys could eat, having triple portions of everything on the diner's menu. Rita tells him that not watching his health will kill him. Phil shrugs her off because he isn't worried about the future.

Illustration: Some day, your metabolism will slow down. (Ice cream—so sweet, so wonderful, so deadly!) God wasn't being a cosmic killjoy when he asked us to dedicate our bodies to him, he was looking out for us. By caring for our health, we can experience all of the sensual pleasures that God created for our enjoyment (within biblical guidelines). Use this scene to help your kids start thinking about taking better care of their bodies.

Questions

- **What kinds of things do people indulge in?**
- **Is physical pleasure a sin? Why or why not?**
- **When does physical pleasure become sin?**
  Read 1 Corinthians 3:16-17.
- **Why is God so concerned about how we treat our bodies?**
- **What do you need to clean from your life to make your temple the best it can be?**

CHANGE—I Have to Give Up What?!

Title: NINE MONTHS (PG-13)

Scripture: Romans 12:2

Alternate Takes: Sacrifice (Hebrews 12:1-2), Selfishness (2 Timothy 3:2-7)

START TIME: *37 minutes, 30 seconds*
START CUE: *Samuel stands next to his Porsche.*
END TIME: *38 minutes, 45 seconds*
END CUE: *Samuel refuses to change his life for the baby.*
DURATION: *1 minute, 15 seconds*

Overview: Samuel can't believe he will have to get rid of his sports car and his elderly cat to accommodate the coming baby. He reminds Rebecca that she promised the baby wouldn't change their lives, so he refuses to change his ways.

Illustration: We've got some sweet marketing going when it comes to salvation (peace, joy, heaven, donuts every Sunday). However, we often leave out the fact that, along with the blessings we receive, we are also asked to clean up all the junk in our lives (a process that *never* ends). Life in Christ is truly wonderful, but it's not always easy. We must be open and willing to adjust our lives at the Spirit's prompting, changing things that will ensure that we grow into healthy children of God.

Questions

- **What is the hardest habit you've had to break? How did you do it?**
- **Why is it so difficult to break habits?**
- **What was the hardest thing to change once you accepted Christ's forgiveness?**
  Read Romans 12:2.
- **Why does God want us to "transform" into Jesus' image?**
- **What is one thing you can do this week to make this change in your life?**

CHANGE—You're So Different!

Title: HOPE FLOATS (PG-13)

Scripture: 2 Corinthians 5:17

Alternate Takes: Forgiveness (Matthew 6:14-15), Pride (James 2:2-8)

START TIME: *31 minutes, 45 seconds*
START CUE: *Birdee interviews with Dot.*
END TIME: *34 minutes, 45 seconds*
END CUE: *Birdee begs Dot for a job.*
DURATION: *3 minutes*

Overview: Birdee barely recognizes Dot, who has changed dramatically since their days in high school together. Birdee apologizes for how she treated Dot in high school, realizing she was probably emotionally cruel to her, and asks forgiveness.

Illustration: People change. Christians should change dramatically as they grow in their relationship with God. Too many believers, however, continue to hang on to their old ways instead of leaving them in the closet for good. The longer we pursue God, the more we should resemble him, daily changing into his image. Get your kids talking about how change isn't just required at the Laundromat, it's also required by God.

Questions
- **What kinds of kids do people make fun of at your school? Why?**
- **How would you feel being interviewed for a job ten years from now by a person you ridiculed in school?**
- **In what ways do people change over the years?**
   Read 2 Corinthians 5:17.
- **How do people see that you've been changed by Jesus?**
- **What old things do you need to throw off this week so the new creation can shine through?**

CHRISTIAN LIFE—All Fixed!

Title: PLEASANTVILLE (PG-13)

Scripture: 2 Corinthians 5:15-17

Alternate Take: Perfection (Romans 3:23)

START TIME: *23 minutes, 00 seconds*
START CUE: *The basketball team practices.*
END TIME: *24 minutes, 15 seconds*
END CUE: *Bud kicks the basketball and swishes it.*
DURATION: *1 minute, 15 seconds*

Overview: The basketball team practices, and every player makes a perfect shot every time. Bud tries several crazy shots (even kicking the ball off the ceiling), and sinks them all.

Illustration: A popular myth is that accepting Christ makes your life perfect. This is not true. (If it is, I got a raw deal!) Faith in Jesus brings meaning and joy to life, but it doesn't smooth out every crease. The sooner you and your students expose this myth, the better.

Questions

- **Do you ever wish you had a perfect life? Why or why not?**
- **Does accepting Jesus make life perfect? Why or why not?**
    Read 2 Corinthians 5:15-17.
- **Even though we are new creations, why do we continue doing stupid, sinful things?**
- **Why doesn't God make everything perfect when we enter his family?**
- **How can you cope with future "imperfections" in your life?**

CHRISTIAN LIFE—Baby Steps

Title: WHAT ABOUT BOB? (PG)

Scripture: Proverbs 27:1

Alternate Take: Trials (1 Peter 1:6-7)

START TIME: *11 minutes, 45 seconds*
START CUE: *Bob says, "You can help me."*
END TIME: *14 minutes, 30 seconds*
END CUE: *Bob leaves Dr. Marvin's office.*
DURATION: *2 minutes, 45 seconds*

Overview: Everything scares Bob. Dr. Marvin helps him cope by explaining the concept of baby steps. Instead of worrying about the entire task, a person should just focus on each little task, one at a time, until the goal is reached. Bob practices by taking baby steps all over the office and finally out the door.

Illustration: We can't control the future. All we can do is focus on the here and now and follow God's will in each moment. Sometimes the path ahead can seem overwhelming. This clip can start a discussion about how, when we take one step at a time with God, he will walk us safely through the valley to the other side.

Questions

- **What is the most overwhelming situation you have ever faced?**
- **How did you get through it?**

Read Proverbs 27:1.
- Why should we take only one step at a time when we're in a difficult situation?
- What guarantee do you have that God will be with you?
- How can you turn your worries about the future into "baby steps" for today?

CHRISTIAN LIFE—E.T. Phone Home!

Title: E.T. THE EXTRA-TERRESTRIAL (PG)

Scripture: John 17:14-16

Alternate Take: Kindness (Matthew 25:34-36)

START TIME: *38 minutes, 00 seconds*
START CUE: *Elliott asks E.T. where his home is.*
END TIME: *39 minutes, 00 seconds*
END CUE: *E.T. points to the stars.*
DURATION: *1 minute*

Overview: Elliott tries to find out where E.T.'s home is by showing him maps and globes. E.T. points to the stars instead, and creates a levitating version of his solar system.

Illustration: As Christians, we are aliens in this world. Though our physical bodies belong here, our spirits belong in heaven. We will remain in this world for a time, but we'll live forever in our true home in heaven with our Father. This scene will get your kids talking about where their home really is!

Questions
- Where was the farthest you have been from home?
- Did you get homesick? Were you unable to communicate with people at home? How did that feel?
  Read John 17:14-16.
- How are we like aliens?
- Do you ever feel like an alien? When?
- What are the priorities of your true home, and how can you incorporate them into your life now?

CHRISTIAN LIFE—Things Change

Title: PLEASANTVILLE (PG-13)

Scripture: 2 Corinthians 3:18

Alternate Take: Salvation (2 Corinthians 5:17)

START TIME: *1 hour, 40 minutes, 00 seconds*
START CUE: *George visits Bud in jail.*
END TIME: *1 hour, 42 minutes, 00 seconds*
END CUE: *Bud and George sit in silence.*
DURATION: *2 minutes*

Overview: Bud's dad, George, visits him in jail. He confesses to Bud that he doesn't like change and asks him when everything went wrong. Bud replies that nothing went wrong, people just change.

Illustration: To follow Christ is to live with constant change. The Holy Spirit lives inside of us and constantly works to mold us into the image of our Lord. This means that every day we change a little bit more. Over the years, our lives will look completely different from where we started our journey with Christ. This clip can get kids talking about how change is good and godly.

Questions
- **What is one thing in your life that you want to stay the same forever? Why?**
- **What is the biggest change you've gone through? What happened?**
  Read 2 Corinthians 3:18.
- **How does this verse guarantee change will happen in your life?**
- **How has your relationship with Jesus changed you? What still needs to change?**
- **What can you do to accelerate the positive changes in your life?**

CHRISTIAN LIFE—The Eternal Melting Pot

Title: SIMON BIRCH (PG)

Scripture: John 3:14-18

Alternate Takes: Judging (1 Corinthians 1:26-29), Faith (Mark 10:13-16)

START TIME: *31 minutes, 15 seconds*
START CUE: *Miss Leavey says, "Didn't your mom teach you to be quiet?"*
END TIME: *32 minutes, 45 seconds*
END CUE: *Joe and Simon fall into the room.*
DURATION: *1 minute, 30 seconds*

Overview: Miss Leavey grills Simon, berating him for misbehaving. She tells him he doesn't belong in church and questions his belief that God will use him. Miss Wenteworth rescues Simon, telling Miss Leavey that Simon has more faith than she will ever understand.

Illustration: You don't get to pick who is in your earthly family, and that goes *double* for your heavenly one. God invites into heaven anyone who repents and begins a relationship with him. That means we must regard *all* of our brothers and sisters, from the golden child to the social outcast, with the same love and reverence. God's table seats many guests, and we should be thankful to be at the table instead of questioning the credentials of the person sitting next to us.

Questions
- **How would you feel if someone said you didn't belong in our church?**
- **What types of people don't deserve entrance into heaven? Why?**
- **What if those people repent and develop a relationship with Jesus?**
  Read John 3:14-18.
- **What qualifications does a person need to have in order to become part of God's family?**
- **How do you need to change your view of your brothers and sisters in Christ?**

CHRISTIAN LIFE—Making a Difference

Title: MR. HOLLAND'S OPUS (PG)

Scripture: Acts 7:54–8:1

Alternate Take: Eternal Rewards (1 Timothy 6:17-19)

START TIME: *2 hours, 8 minutes, 30 seconds*
START CUE: *Iris motions for everyone to sit down.*
END TIME: *2 hour, 11 minutes, 15 seconds*
END CUE: *Miss Lang says, "We are the music of your life."*
DURATION: *2 minutes, 45 seconds*

Overview: People jam-pack the school auditorium to honor the life of Mr. Holland. His former student and current governor Miss Lang gives a moving tribute to the man who impacted her as a teen. She says that Mr. Holland touched every one of his students and that, even though he may not have finished composing his musical symphony, his students represent his living symphony.

Illustration: I got choked up just writing about the scene. (Good thing my wife thinks that's sweet.) A servant's life doesn't often fill the wall with awards or the bank account with C-notes, but its eternal worth is priceless. We may never know the far-reaching ramifications of helping people and making a difference in their lives here on earth, but the spiritual impact is worth the physical sacrifice.

Questions
- **Who has impacted your life the most?**
- **Do they know how much they've done for you? Why or why not?**
- **How should people judge their spiritual success in life?**
  Read Acts 7:54–8:1.
- **How did Stephen's life impact the world in ways he never knew?**
- **How can you motivate yourself to continue to serve others even when it seems like nothing is changing?**

CHRISTIAN LIFE—Where's the Fun?

Title: HAPPY GILMORE (PG-13)

Scripture: Ecclesiastes 5:18-19

Alternate Take: Sanctification (James 4:8-10)

START TIME: *42 minutes, 15 seconds*
START CUE: *Virginia confronts Happy about his behavior.*
END TIME: *43 minutes, 00 seconds*
END CUE: *Happy agrees to change his ways.*
DURATION: *45 seconds*

Overview: Virginia tells Happy that he can't cuss, fight, or throw his clubs anymore if he wants to play golf. Happy complains that she's taking away all of the fun. Virginia disagrees, telling him that he can still be crazy and wild—within reason. Happy agrees to tone down his wild behavior.

Illustration: This is the way that many of people think of Christianity—it's no fun! Satan promotes the idea that Christians can't do anything fun; but he forgets to tell us that the restrictions actually help us to enjoy life *more* than if we indulged our every whim. Help your teenagers discover that God wants our lives to be a blast!

Questions
- **What things did you have to give up when you became a Christian?**
- **Why do some people think Christians can't have fun?**
  Read Ecclesiastes 5:18-19.
- **Why does God want us to enjoy life?**
- **How do rules allow you to have more fun in life than you would have doing whatever you want?**
- **How can you change the perception that Christians don't have fun?**

CHRISTIANESE—Say What?

Title: HAPPY GILMORE (PG-13)

Scripture: Acts 1:8

Alternate Take: Holy Spirit (1 Corinthians 2:10-14)

START TIME: *35 minutes, 00 seconds*
START CUE: *Happy and Gary meet.*
END TIME: *35 minutes, 45 seconds*
END CUE: *Happy says, "Psycho."*
DURATION: *45 seconds*

Themes A-C

Overview: Gary tries to teach Happy about repelling negative energy and harnessing positive energy to improve his golf game. Happy looks at him like he's speaking a different language.

Illustration: Gary's explanation sounds like it's from another world. Unfortunately, Christians can sometimes sound just as strange when speaking "Christian code" around pre-believers. People who don't grow up in the church have no idea what words like "saved" and "sanctify" mean. We must be aware of exclusive phrases and strive to include everyone in our conversations. This clip will help your students realize how important it is to communicate the good news in a clear way.

Questions
- **What is the weirdest spiritual belief someone has shared with you?**
- **Have you ever talked to someone and had no idea what they were saying? What happened?**
  Read Acts 1:8.
- **What does it mean to be a witness?**
- **Why is it so important to communicate clearly?**
- **What Christian phrases can be confusing to non-Christians? What words can you use instead that aren't so confusing?**

THE CHURCH—One Special Job

Title: GALAXY QUEST (PG)

Scripture: 1 Corinthians 12:12-27

Alternate Take: Work (Colossians 3:23-24)

START TIME: *42 minutes, 15 seconds*
START CUE: *The crew tries to assess the ship's damage.*
END TIME: *43 minutes, 30 seconds*
END CUE: *Tawny finishes her outburst.*
DURATION: *1 minute, 15 seconds*

Overview: Taggart tries to determine the extent of the damage to the ship. The computer only responds, though, when Tawny asks it questions. When the computer answers, Tawny repeats exactly what the computer just said. Laredo tells Tawny she's annoying, and she responds that her one job may be stupid, but she's going to do it right.

Illustration: Some people feel like the earlobe in the body of Christ. Not every job is as flashy as the pastor or worship leader, but every part is crucial for the body to function properly. This clip can be a great tool to help your kids discover their part in the body of Christ.

Questions
- Have you ever been part of a team and had a seemingly unimportant job? What was it like?
- What would have happened if you hadn't done your job?
    Read 1 Corinthians 12:12-27.
- What are some behind-the-scenes jobs that need to be done for church to happen every week?
- What would happen if a part of the church body decided to quit?
- How can you do your part to help the church body function better?

COMPASSION—It's Not My Problem

Title: STAR WARS: EPISODE 1— THE PHANTOM MENACE (PG)

Scripture: Matthew 15:22-28

Alternate Takes: Sin (James 4:17), Forgiveness (Matthew 18:21-22), Community (Joshua 7:1-13)

START TIME: *14 minutes, 45 seconds*
START CUE: *Qui-Gon and Obi-Wan meet Boss Nass.*
END TIME: *16 minutes, 00 seconds*
END CUE: *Boss Nass sends the Jedi away.*
DURATION: *1 minute, 15 seconds*

Overview: Qui-Gon and Obi-Wan ask the Gungan ruler Boss Nass to help them warn the Naboo of impending danger. Boss Nass responds that they don't care about the haughty Naboo since the Gungans are safe in their underwater home. Obi-Wan cautions that whatever happens to one affects the other, but Boss Nass will not listen.

Illustration: Never ask a computer-generated character for help. With the proliferation of computers and cell phones, our lives have become increasingly more self-contained. This self-reliance has hurt our perspective on caring for others. We think, "If I can do it on my own, why can't other people?" Yet Jesus calls us to look upon every person with compassion, the same way he looks upon us.

Questions

- **When was the last time you showed compassion to someone? What happened?**

  Read Matthew 15:22-28.

- **Why would Jesus say something that sounds so unloving? Did he end up showing love?**

- **What does this passage reveal about the relationship between Jews and Gentiles in Jesus' culture? Are there similar cultural issues in our society today?**

- **Who should we show compassion to? What opportunities to show compassion are you overlooking in your everyday life?**

- **How can you show compassion to someone this week?**

Themes A-C

CONFESSION–Caught Red-Handed!

Title: NOTTING HILL (PG-13)

Scripture: Proverbs 28:13

Alternate Takes: Stealing (Exodus 20:15), Lying (Proverbs 13:5)

START TIME: *7 minutes, 00 seconds*
START CUE: *William sees the thief on camera.*
END TIME: *8 minutes, 15 seconds*
END CUE: *William returns to Anna.*
DURATION: *1 minute, 15 seconds*

Overview: William catches a man stealing from his bookstore. He confronts the man, who refuses to admit his guilt even when he's caught red-handed.

Illustration: It's hard to admit when we're wrong. I mean, some people *still* haven't admitted that *Flashdance* fashion was a horrible mistake. The basis of our faith, though, is admitting we are wrong—confessing that we're sinners. Use this clip to get kids talking about how confession leads to true forgiveness.

Questions

- **Have you ever seen someone get caught doing something wrong? What happened?**

- **Have you ever acted like the thief in the video? Why?**

- **Why is admitting we're wrong so hard?**
  Read Proverbs 28:13.
- **Why is confession so important to God?**
- **How can you make confession a more natural part of your life?**

CONFLICT—Shootout at Sundown

Title: THE SURE THING (PG-13)

Scripture: Ephesians 4:26-27

Alternate Take: Taming the Tongue (1 Thessalonians 5:11)

START TIME: *26 minutes, 45 seconds*
START CUE: *Gib gets into the car.*
END TIME: *28 minutes*
END CUE: *Gary starts the car and sings "The Age of Aquarius."*
DURATION: *1 minute, 15 seconds*

Overview: Gib and Alison greet each other with hostility and with snide, hurtful remarks, having never resolved their differences.

Illustration: Only professional wrestlers enjoy conflict! Most people allow unresolved anger to fester rather than dealing with it. In this clip, Gib and Alison are Exhibit A for unresolved problems. Yet God is very direct on this subject: Deal with it. Until you do, an unresolved problem strains earthly and spiritual relationships.

Questions
- **Tell about your worst unresolved conflict. What happened?**
- **Why does it sometimes seem easiest to avoid solving a problem?**
  Read Ephesians 4:26-27.
- **Why does God encourage us to resolve conflict immediately? What are the benefits of doing this?**
- **Does conflict impact our spiritual life? How?**
- **What is one way you can heal unresolved conflict this week?**

CONFLICT—Wanna Piece of Me?

Title: WILLIAM SHAKESPEARE'S ROMEO + JULIET (PG-13)

Scripture: Matthew 5:38-39

Alternate Take: Persecution (Matthew 5:10-12)

START TIME: *1 hour, 00 minutes*
START CUE: *Tybalt challenges Romeo.*

END TIME: *1 hour, 2 minutes, 30 seconds*
END CUE: *Tybalt hits and kicks Romeo.*
DURATION: *2 minutes, 30 seconds*

Overview: Tybalt wants to fight Romeo. Romeo, however, turns the other cheek, excusing Tybalt's harsh words and punishing fists and pleading with him to forgive and forget. Tybalt refuses and beats up Romeo, who offers no defense.

Illustration: This violent scene shows the honor and peril of turning the other cheek. Jesus commands us to extend love to everyone, even enemies who won't accept it. This difficult teaching would be easy to ignore if Jesus hadn't lived it out for our salvation.

Questions
- **Was Romeo smart to not fight back? Why or why not?**
- **What risks did he take in refusing to fight?**
- **Have you ever been in a situation where you turned the other cheek to someone? What happened?**
  Read Matthew 5:38-39.
- **Why does Jesus command us to turn the other cheek?**
- **How can you turn the other cheek to people this week?**

CONFRONTATION—What Were You Thinking?

Title: EMMA (PG)

Scripture: Matthew 18:15

Alternate Take: Compassion (Zechariah 7:9-10)

START TIME: *1 hour, 31 minutes, 00 seconds*
START CUE: *Mr. Knightley catches up to Emma.*
END TIME: *1 hour, 33 minutes, 00 seconds*
END CUE: *Mr. Knightley leaves Emma alone.*
DURATION: *2 minutes*

Overview: Mr. Knightley confronts Emma about tearing Miss Bates down. Emma tries to brush it off, but Knightley refuses to let it go. He makes Emma see the wrong she has done to Miss Bates.

Illustration: Most people hate being told they're wrong, and few people like to confront others with the wrong they've done. Yet God's Word encourages Christians to point out one another's missteps when necessary—not in judgment, but in love. Though it may hurt sometimes, it helps the body remain healthy and grow stronger.

Questions
- **Have you ever had to confront someone? What happened?**

- **Why is confrontation so hard?**
  Read Matthew 18:15.
- **Why can't we just let God convict Christians of their sins and not get involved?**
- **Is there a way to confront someone without being judgmental? How?**
- **How can you build relationships that allow for loving confrontation?**

CONSEQUENCES—The Imperfect Crime

Title: WILLY WONKA AND THE CHOCOLATE FACTORY (G)

Scripture: John 8:34-36

Alternate Take: Disobedience (Titus 1:13-16)

START TIME: *1 hour, 11 minutes, 15 seconds*
START CUE: *Violet picks up the piece of gum.*
END TIME: *1 hour, 13 minutes, 00 seconds*
END CUE: *The Oompa-Loompas roll (blueberry) Violet away.*
DURATION: *1 minute, 45 seconds*

Overview: Willy Wonka shows the children his experimental chewing gum that tastes like a full-course meal. Violet chews a piece, even though Mr. Wonka tells her not to. Violet loves the gum until she gets to "dessert" and turns into a human blueberry.

Illustration: Why do we always have to touch the hot stove for ourselves? (If you never have, you're missing out!) Violet learns immediately what comes with disobedience—consequences! Even though some consequences may not occur for years, they eventually catch up with us. This clip about consequences will help your students dig deeper into a topic they may not often consider.

Questions
- **Have you ever done something that had immediate consequences? What happened?**
- **Why do we still do things even when people warn us of the consequences?**
  Read John 8:34-36.
- **How does sin make you a slave?**
- **How should you deal with the consequences of past mistakes?**
- **What are you doing now that will have bad consequences in the future?**

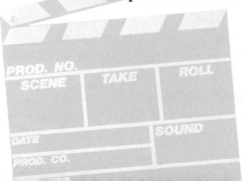

CONTENTMENT—I Love My Job!

Title: SO I MARRIED AN AXE MURDERER (PG-13)

Scripture: Philippians 2:14-16

Alternate Takes: Expectations (Matthew 20:1-16), Thankfulness (Colossians 3:15-17)

START TIME: *16 minutes, 30 seconds*
START CUE: *The police captain walks up.*
END TIME: *18 minutes, 00 seconds*
END CUE: *The captain says he will try to be meaner.*
DURATION: *1 minute, 30 seconds*

Overview: A cop complains to his captain that he always dreamed of the thrill, danger, and adventure of police work. Instead, paperwork and boredom fill his days. He asks the captain to yell at him more so he can feel like the reckless cops on TV who always get in trouble.

Illustration: Everybody has duties—school, a job, sports, church, chores, or extracurricular activities. Even though these may start out fun, the glamour can wear off and boredom can easily set in. Few people find true contentment with life, and instead they long for a fantasy life instead of enjoying reality. Use this scene to help your students realize that God wants us to be content and rest in him *now*, trusting that he has us in the best place.

Questions
- **What is the most boring thing you have ever had to do?**
- **Is anything you do exciting *all the time*?**
- **How do people usually respond to boredom? What are some good ways to deal with it?**
    Read Philippians 2:14-16.
- **How can you keep yourself from complaining or arguing?**
- **How can you find contentment in the boring times of life?**

CONTENTMENT—Hurry Up Already!

Title: THE EMPIRE STRIKES BACK (PG)

Scripture: Psalm 139:1-16

Alternate Takes: Patience (Colossians 1:10-12), Judging (John 7:24)

START TIME: *54 minutes, 00 seconds*
START CUE: *Luke sits in Yoda's hovel.*
END TIME: *57 minutes, 00 seconds*

END CUE: *Luke pleads with Yoda.*
DURATION: *3 minutes*

Overview: Luke pleads with Yoda to introduce him to the great Jedi Master. Luke becomes frustrated with waiting and finally blows up. Then he realizes that Yoda *is* the Jedi Master he was seeking. Yoda believes Luke is too impatient, angry, and discontent to be trained. Luke had been looking to the future and better times instead of dealing with where he was at the time.

Illustration: Few people are content. (How often do you hear, "I can't wait until summer?") People live with their focus on the future—going to college, getting their own apartment, or having more money—instead of living in the here and now. God desires faithfulness with the duties he gives us. This scene will jump-start a discussion about how contentment and diligence in the present brings greater responsibilities in the future.

Questions
- **What are you looking forward to most in the future?**
- **Does it ever distract you and make you discontent with the present? Why?**
- **What things might you miss out on now by focusing too much on the future?**
    Read Psalm 139:1-16.
- **How does it make you feel to know that God ordained every day of your life—even this day?**
- **What do you need to do to become more content with your life?**

COURAGE—You Don't Scare Me!

Title: THE WIZARD OF OZ (G)

Scripture: Joshua 1:9

Alternate Takes: Cowardice (Exodus 32:19-24), Kindness (Hebrews 13:2)

START TIME: *49 minutes, 00 seconds*
START CUE: *The Cowardly Lion appears.*
END TIME: *51 minutes, 00 seconds*
END CUE: *The Cowardly Lion bursts into tears.*
DURATION: *2 minutes*

Overview: The Cowardly Lion bounds out of the forest to terrorize Dorothy and the others. When they finally fight against the lion's intimidation, his true cowardly nature comes out for all to see.

Illustration: There's not much surprise as to this character's true nature when his first name is Cowardly! Christians often appear as meek as this lion. A follower of Christ should have the courage of a hundred lions, since we have the power of the Creator behind us. Use this clip to help your kids discover how God gives us a spirit of strength and power!

Questions
- Have you ever felt like the Cowardly Lion? When?
- Why do situations like that frighten you?
- When is your faith timid or cowardly?
    Read Joshua 1:9.
- Why should we not be afraid in terrifying situations?
- What are some specific ways you can begin to live more courageously?

COVETOUSNESS—I Want It Now!

Title: WILLY WONKA AND THE CHOCOLATE FACTORY (G)

Scripture: 1 Timothy 6:9-11

Alternate Takes: Contentment (1 Timothy 6:6-8), Patience (Ecclesiastes 7:8)

START TIME: *1 hour, 20 minutes, 15 seconds*
START CUE: *Veruca tells her father she wants a golden goose.*
END TIME: *1 hour, 23 minutes, 00 seconds*
END CUE: *Mr. Salt jumps after his daughter.*
DURATION: *2 minutes, 45 seconds*

Overview: Willy Wonka shows his tour group the geese that lay golden chocolate eggs. Veruca Salt tells her dad to buy her one. When Mr. Wonka refuses to sell, Veruca lists all the things she wants *now*!

Illustration: *Warning!* This clip contains singing by bad girl Veruca Salt. Though we rarely voice our every desire, our eyes constantly shop around, desiring much that we see. Contentment may not be part of the American Dream, but it is a big part of God's plan. This clip is a great platform to help your students dive in to issues such as greed and materialism.

Questions
- Have you ever wanted something immediately after seeing it? What happened?
- How would you describe the American Dream?
    Read 1 Timothy 6:9-11.
- When is it wrong to want something?
- How does greed affect people?
- What is one thing that you covet and how can you stop wanting it?

COVETOUSNESS—That Looks Good!

Title: PEE-WEE'S BIG ADVENTURE (PG)

Scripture: Exodus 20:17

Alternate Takes: Taming the Tongue (1 Thessalonians 5:11), Contentment (1 Timothy 6:6-8)

START TIME: *10 minutes, 00 seconds*
START CUE: *Pee-Wee walks up to Francis.*
END TIME: *11 minutes, 45 seconds*
END CUE: *Pee-Wee rides away on his bike.*
DURATION: *1 minute, 45 seconds*

Overview: Francis wants to buy Pee-Wee Herman's beloved bike because it's all he can think about. Pee-Wee refuses, and they get into a childish name-calling contest.

Illustration: Covetousness, perhaps the least understood topic in the Ten Commandments, can really gnaw at our hearts! This silly scene can help start a discussion about how our consumer-oriented society promotes covetousness and undermines contentment.

Questions

- **As a kid, what toy did you want most but couldn't have?**
- **Why do you think Francis doesn't want a different bike?**
- **When does wanting something become sin?**
  Read Exodus 20:17.
- **What is covetousness?**
- **How can you overcome covetous desires?**

Movie Illustration
THEMES D-F
Dating...Faith...The Future...

DATING—Desperately Waiting for "The One"

Title: NEVER BEEN KISSED (PG-13)

Scripture: Psalm 37:3-4

Alternate Take: Passion (Song of Songs 3:5)

START TIME: *5 minutes, 00 seconds*
START CUE: *Josie says, "The right guy is out there."*
END TIME: *6 minutes, 15 seconds*
END CUE: *Josie says, "You're so scared it will go away."*
DURATION: *1 minute, 15 seconds*

Overview: Josie tells her friends that she's not going to kiss a bunch of losers to find the right guy. She's going to save herself for that one special guy who'll sweep her off her feet and kiss her like none other.

Illustration: Relationships (even marriages) are so disposable these days, and the social necessity of being in a relationship is incredibly high. God doesn't want it to be that way. By resting in his love and gaining self-worth from him, you can wait patiently for the special person God has for you and save yourself a ton of hassle along the way.

Questions
- **Do you agree with what Josie said? Why or why not?**
- **Why do people end up kissing a lot of losers instead of waiting for that one special person?**
- **Do you think there's only one perfect person out there for you? Why or why not?**
  Read Psalm 37:3-4.
- **How does God make waiting easier?**
- **How can you weed out the losers in your life and become more patient?**

DATING—Eenie, Meenie...

Title: BETTER OFF DEAD (PG)

Scripture: Proverbs 31:10-31

Alternate Takes: Pride (Colossians 3:12-14), Rejection (Genesis 29:30-31)

START TIME: *41 minutes, 45 seconds*
START CUE: *Lane picks up Joanne.*
END TIME: *43 minutes, 15 seconds*
END CUE: *Lane writes Joanne a check.*
DURATION: *1 minute, 30 seconds*

Overview: Lane Myer picks up Joanne Greenwald for a date. Lane considers Joanne "beneath him," but his dad makes him take her out. Surprisingly, Joanne thinks Lane is a loser and charges him what her dinner would have cost instead of going out with him.

Illustration: Arranged marriage has gone the way of Pogs. (Thank you, Lord! My parents would've chosen a nice, proper young lady with perfected piano skills, not my rockin' bride.) Unfortunately, most teens now base their selections on attraction alone, not on biblical standards. Friends and MTV pressure kids to look at the outside and disregard the inside. This clip will spark a great discussion about dating.

Questions
- **What is the most uncomfortable dating experience you've ever had? What happened?**
- **Why did you go out with that person in the first place?**
  Read Proverbs 31:10-31.
- **What characteristics does the woman in this passage have? What qualities should a potential date have?**
- **How can this passage help you make your dating choices?**
- **How can you become more patient and wait for a person with those qualities?**

DATING—She Loves Me Not

Title: DUMB AND DUMBER (PG-13)

Scripture: Psalm 34:17-18

Alternate Take: Honesty (Hebrews 13:18)

START TIME: *1 hour, 31 minutes, 00 seconds*
START CUE: *Lloyd professes his love to Mary.*
END TIME: *1 hour, 32 minutes, 30 seconds*
END CUE: *Lloyd is excited because he has a "chance" at love with Mary.*
DURATION: *1 minute, 30 seconds*

Overview: Lloyd professes his undying love to Mary. He asks what his chances are with her, and she replies about a million to one (side note: she did decide to marry the guy in real life). Lloyd rejoices in the fact that he has a shot with the woman of his dreams.

Illustration: Hopeless romantics unite! There's always one person out there who has no problem walking up to someone, declaring his or her interest, and immediately receiving affirmation. The rest of us suffer through life wracked with uncertainty and terror surrounding our decision to voice our lovin' feelings. Thankfully, God is always there to mend our broken heart!

Questions
- What has been your worst experience with rejection?
- How did you get over it?
- Have you ever rejected someone? What happened? How did they deal with it?
  Read Psalm 34:17-18.
- How can God help you through times of rejection and heartache?
- How can you exhibit the love of Christ, even when you have to tell someone that you're not interested in him or her?

DATING—That'll Leave a Mark

Title: THAT THING YOU DO! (PG)

Scripture: Proverbs 4:23

Alternate Takes: Forgiveness (Ephesians 4:31-32), Taming the Tongue (James 3:8-12)

START TIME: *1 hour, 25 minutes, 45 seconds*
START CUE: *Jimmy and Faye talk in the dressing room.*
END TIME: *1 hour, 28 minutes, 15 seconds*
END CUE: *Mr. White says, "The same person who said you had class."*
DURATION: *2 minutes, 30 seconds*

Overview: Jimmy rips into his girlfriend Faye because the TV crew announced their engagement during his live performance. Faye, holding back the tears, breaks up with him, claiming she should never have wasted her love on a man who didn't love her back.

Illustration: Breaking up is no fun. (Keep it under ten minutes. Trust me.) The end of a relationship is a good reminder that when you enter a relationship you should guard your heart. Keeping yourself from going too far emotionally (giving your heart completely to someone) before you're ready to make a lifelong commitment is almost as important as guarding yourself physically. This clip can start an honest discussion about how guarding yourself physically in romance is extremely important, but emotional scars can be damaging too.

Questions
- Have you ever felt like Faye did? Why?
- In hindsight, do broken relationships seem like a waste of time? Why or why not?
  Read Proverbs 4:23.
- What does "guarding your heart" mean?
- Why does God encourage us to do that?
- What are specific ways you can guard your heart in your dating life?

DEATH—A Sure Thing

Title: WHAT ABOUT BOB? (PG)

Scripture: Romans 6:23

Alternate Take: Afterlife (John 3:14-18)

START TIME: *58 minutes, 15 seconds*
START CUE: *Siggy and Bob lie in their beds.*
END TIME: *59 minutes, 15 seconds*
END CUE: *Siggy asks, "What else is there to be afraid of?"*
DURATION: *1 minute*

Overview: Siggy asks Bob if he's afraid of death. Everybody dies, and Siggy, all of twelve years old, can't stop thinking about it.

Illustration: At age twelve, I was trying to finish my *Star Wars* card collection, not obsessing about death! Yet death does affect everyone, from observing other people's deaths to facing our own. We don't often talk about it, though. Use this clip to get your kids thinking about this deeply felt issue. After all, while Christians shouldn't have a death wish, they shouldn't fear death either.

Questions
- **Have you ever been to a funeral? How did you feel?**
- **Why do you think people are so afraid of death?**
  Read Romans 6:23.
- **What is the root cause of death?**
- **What will happen when you die?**
- **How should a Christian view death?**

DIRECTION—Which Way's North?

Title: MUPPET TREASURE ISLAND (G)

Scripture: Isaiah 58:11

Alternate Takes: The Bible (Psalm 19:7-11), Sharing Our Hurts (2 Corinthians 7:6-7)

START TIME: *37 minutes, 15 seconds*
START CUE: *Jim asks where north is.*
END TIME: *38 minutes, 45 seconds*
END CUE: *Jim puts away his compass.*
DURATION: *1 minute, 30 seconds*

Overview: Jim and Long John Silver look at the stars. Jim says he can locate north with his compass, but he has no clue how to find it otherwise. Long

John Silver says he doesn't follow rules and regulations, but instead he uses the stars, because then he can always find north.

Illustration: It might be hard to relate to this scene, with GPS units practically wristwatch-sized nowadays, but its truth remains: Everyone needs direction in life. The problem is that everyone has his or her own method for finding north (and even "north" sometimes seems to be negotiable). Use this scene to help your students determine "true north" and discover how to follow it.

Questions
- **What different ways do people use to navigate through life?**
- **What's your compass in life?**
  Read Isaiah 58:11.
- **How can you be sure that God will lead you in the right direction?**
- **Why doesn't God always make the path clear and obvious?**
- **What things can you do to help you stay on course in life?**

DISCERNMENT—Do You Hear What I Hear?

Title: THE MISSION (PG)

Scripture: Psalm 103:6-8

Alternate Take: Allegiance (Matthew 6:24)

START TIME: *1 hour, 21 minutes, 15 seconds*
START CUE: *The cardinal tells the natives to return to the jungle.*
END TIME: *1 hour, 23 minutes, 15 seconds*
END CUE: *The natives leave.*
DURATION: *2 minutes*

Overview: The cardinal tells the natives that they must leave the mission, the home they helped build. He declares that it's God's will for them to leave. The chief questions the cardinal's ability to hear God, believing he listens instead to men.

Illustration: I am constantly amazed at how God supposedly speaks to one person concerning another. It doesn't seem to me that God would need a middleman. This scene can prompt a discussion of God's will—how do you know what it is? How do you hear God? How do you discern if someone is speaking to you out of selfish ambition or through God's leading? Though you may never have a burning-bush experience, the more intimate you are with God, the more clearly his voice will sound.

Questions

- **How would you feel if you were one of the natives?**
  Read Psalm 103:6-8.
- **Does God still make his will clear to people as he did to Moses and the people of Israel? What are some of the ways he communicates with us?**
- **How can you know if it is really God speaking to you? to someone else?**
- **How do you follow God's will, even when it doesn't make sense to you?**
- **What do you believe is God's will for your life right now, and how are you following it?**

DIVORCE—Falling Out of Love

Title: STEPMOM (PG-13)

Scripture: 1 John 4:7-11

Alternate Takes: Rationalizing Sin (Proverbs 21:2), Love (1 Corinthians 13)

START TIME: *16 minutes, 00 seconds*
START CUE: *Luke puts Ben's model boat in the water.*
END TIME: *18 minutes, 00 seconds*
END CUE: *Luke finishes talking with his kids.*
DURATION: *2 minutes*

Overview: Luke explains to his children why he and their mom got a divorce. He sugarcoats the issue by saying that they still love each other, but it's a different kind of love. Naturally, the children don't understand and want him to get back together with their mom.

Illustration: Most reasons for divorce are like people's feet—everybody's got them, and they all stink! Children often hear the lamest excuses and get a warped sense of what love should be. God's love, however, never wavers and never leaves. Use this clip to help your teenagers discover that no matter what happens on earth, God's love for them remains constant.

Questions

- **What is your definition of love?**
- **Why should you not "fall out of love" with your spouse?**
  Read 1 John 4:7-11.
- **How is God's love different from earthly love?**
- **What does God's unconditional love mean to you?**
- **How can you build this love into your life now and into your future marriage?**

DIVORCE—What Did He Say?!

Title: HOPE FLOATS (PG-13)

Scripture: Genesis 2:22-24

Alternate Takes: Forgiveness (Ephesians 4:31–5:2), Parents (Ephesians 6:1-4)

START TIME: *27 minutes, 00 seconds*
START CUE: *Birdee confronts Bernice about talking to her dad.*
END TIME: *27 minutes, 45 seconds*
END CUE: *Grandmother gets into the fight with Birdee and Bernice.*
DURATION: *45 seconds*

Overview: Birdee yells at her daughter Bernice for revealing Birdee's misery to her ex-husband. Bernice complains that Birdee doesn't care about her anymore, and that she just feels sorry for herself.

Illustration: I wish we didn't need to have any illustrations for a talk about divorce, but I can't turn a blind eye to this epidemic. Too many people relate to the bickering and manipulation in this scene. The pain and betrayal among family members is acute and difficult to overcome. Thankfully God can and will repair the damage, but it will take considerable time.

Questions
- **How many of you related to this clip?**
- **How did you deal with being in the middle of fighting parents?**
  Read Genesis 2:22-24.
- **Does divorce prove that people become one flesh? Why or why not?**
- **How can you forgive people who hurt you and each other so much? Have you?**
- **What are you going to do differently in your future marriage?**

DREAMS—You Can Do It!

Title: PEE-WEE'S BIG ADVENTURE (PG)

Scripture: Psalm 37:4

Alternate Takes: Action (Proverbs 6:9-11), Faith (Psalm 37:28)

START TIME: *46 minutes, 30 seconds*
START CUE: *Pee-Wee and Simone sit in the jaws of a dinosaur.*
END TIME: *49 minutes, 00 seconds*
END CUE: *Pee-Wee and Simone watch the sunrise.*
DURATION: *2 minutes, 30 seconds*

Overview: Simone confides in Pee-Wee Herman her dream of traveling to Paris. Pee-Wee encourages her, but she lists all of the reasons she can't. Pee-Wee responds that dreams come true for people who chase them.

Illustration: Everyone has a dream (we're not talking about the one where you go to school in your underwear), but, because of fear or laziness, few dreams come true. God places dreams within us, and he wants to join us on the exciting journey of realizing them. Blessings come by stepping out in faith and by trusting in God's provision.

Questions
- **Was Pee-Wee's advice to Simone right?**
- **What is your dream?**
- **What things are keeping you from achieving your dream?**
  Read Psalm 37:4.
- **Where should the desires of your heart come from? How can you keep your dreams in line with what God wants?**
- **What can you do to make your dream come true?**

ETERNAL REWARDS—What Will Last?

Title: NOTTING HILL (PG-13)

Scripture: Luke 12:16-21

Alternate Takes: Helping Others (Philippians 2:3-5), Beauty (Proverbs 31:30), Contentment (1 Timothy 6:6-8)

START TIME: *42 minutes, 30 seconds*
START CUE: *Anna wants a chance to win the brownie.*
END TIME: *44 minutes, 00 seconds*
END CUE: *Anna loses the brownie.*
DURATION: *1 minute, 30 seconds*

Overview: Anna eats dinner with William and his family. They decide that the person with the worst life story will receive the last brownie. Anna, a world-famous actress, tells her "sad" story of the pitfalls of superstardom, hoping to win.

Illustration: Let's all feel sorry for Anna/Julia Roberts. At least she admits in this scene the fleeting nature of fame, beauty, and fortune. God's Word affirms that only those things that are eternal (like *I Love Lucy* reruns) will never lose their luster and fade away. People who pursue the spiritual aspects of life build lasting treasure.

Questions
- **What would you do if you were a rich and famous movie star?**
- **Why aren't people content with worldly treasures?**
    Read Luke 12:16-21.
- **What does it mean to be "rich toward God"?**
- **What do you treasure in life?**
- **What are some worthy things to begin investing your life in?**

FAILURE—Nooooooo!

Title: PARENTHOOD (PG-13)

Scripture: Psalm 40:1-5

Alternate Takes: Blame (Job 1:13-22),
Good Intentions (1 Kings 8:17-19),
Prayer (1 John 5:14-15),
Trials (James 1:2-4)

START TIME: *45 minutes, 00 seconds*
START CUE: *Gil prays that they will win the game.*
END TIME: *46 minutes, 30 seconds*
END CUE: *Kevin runs away.*
DURATION: *1 minute, 30 seconds*

Overview: Gil's Little League team is about to win its first game. A pop fly goes to his son Kevin, and Kevin drops the ball. The team loses the game and everyone blames Kevin, who blames Gil for putting him in at second base in the first place.

Illustration: Everybody ends up feeling like the goat at some time in life, and it ain't fun chewin' on tin cans! Get your teens talking about how life is full of setbacks and traumas, but that God is there to pick us up, heal our wounds, and get us on our way again.

Questions
- **What do you think has been your biggest failure?**
- **How did you recover?**
    Read Psalm 40:1-5.
- **Did David have failures in his life? How did he deal with them?**
- **How do you deal with failure? How does this Scripture affect how you'll deal with failures in the future?**
- **How can we help one another overcome failure?**

FAITH–D'oh!

Title: TITANIC (PG-13)

Scripture: Psalm 115:1-13

Alternate Takes: Pride (Proverbs 16:18),
God's Creation (Job 38)

START TIME: *22 minutes, 00 seconds*
START CUE: *Rose exits her carriage.*
END TIME: *22 minutes, 45 seconds*
END CUE: *Rose and Cal leave to board the Titanic.*
DURATION: *45 seconds*

Overview: Rose and her fiancé, Cal, gaze upon the Titanic for the first time. Rose comments that it does not look so grand. Cal scoffs at her, saying "God himself could not sink that ship."

Illustration: If this movie were a comedy, we'd cut directly to the Titanic's deep-six. God could and did sink the Titanic, proving we should be careful what we place our faith in. Though it is easier to trust things we can see and touch, our ultimate faith must remain in God. Use this scene to show teenagers that faith in anything other than God usually results in a "shipwreck."

Questions
- **What types of things do people place their faith in?**
- **What will eventually happen to them?**
  Read Psalm 115:1-13.
- **Why do we so often place faith in objects rather than in God?**
- **Have you ever placed too much faith in something other than God? What happened?**
- **What are some ways you can build your faith in God, and not things, this week?**

FAITH–Flying by Faith

Title: SIX DAYS, SEVEN NIGHTS (PG-13)

Scripture: Romans 1:17

Alternate Take: Peer Pressure (Deuteronomy 13:6-8)

START TIME: *5 minutes, 45 seconds*
START CUE: *Robin walks up to the airplane.*
END TIME: *7 minutes, 15 seconds*
END CUE: *Robin and Frank decide to take the plane.*
DURATION: *1 minute, 30 seconds*

Overview: Robin and Frank survey Quinn's plane, questioning its ability to fly since it obviously leaks oil and appears to be decades old. Quinn tells them to trust him, especially since there isn't any other plane available.

Illustration: At times we must place faith in things that appear unworthy. God calls us out on a limb to place our faith in him and his providence. This scene can help you dig deeper with your kids and explore how taking risks of faith can sometimes feel like climbing onto a leaking airplane. Though God won't let us crash, it can sometimes be a scary ride.

Questions
- **Would you have gotten on that plane? Why or why not?**
- **Have you ever placed your faith in something "shaky"? What happened?** Read Romans 1:17.
- **Why does God ask us to live by faith?**
- **Has God ever asked you to place your faith in him when you were unsure? What happened?**
- **How does God ask you to live by faith right now in your life?**

FAITH—Grows Like a Tree

Title: A BUG'S LIFE (G)

Scripture: 2 Thessalonians 1:3-4

Alternate Take: Perseverance (James 1:2-4)

START TIME: *6 minutes, 30 seconds*
START CUE: *Dot catches up to Flik.*
END TIME: *7 minutes, 45 seconds*
END CUE: *Flik walks away from Dot.*
DURATION: *1 minute, 15 seconds*

Overview: Dot complains to Flik about her underdeveloped wings. She wants to fly now! Flik encourages her, showing her that a seed that starts out small eventually grows into a towering tree—it only takes time and patience.

Illustration: Faith begins small and grows larger and stronger. By trusting God with the small things and watching him answer, our faith grows stronger. We start to place increased faith in him and his goodness, giving over more and more areas of our life until it all rests in his hands. It takes small steps of faith to give us the faith to walk on water (or to fly!).

Questions
- **Have you ever tried to "fly" too soon? What happened?**
- **How is faith like the seed in the movie clip?**

Read 2 Thessalonians 1:3-4.

- **What things cause faith to grow? to wilt?**
- **What specific situations in your life have caused your faith to grow?**
- **What does God want you to trust him with today so that your faith will grow?**

FAITH—My Dad Can Beat Up Your Dad!

Title: STAR WARS (PG)

Scripture: Psalm 20:7-8

Alternate Takes: Pride (Proverbs 27:1-2),
Taming the Tongue (1 Samuel 2:3)

START TIME: *36 minutes, 30 seconds*
START CUE: *Admiral Motti brags about the Death Star.*
END TIME: *38 minutes, 30 seconds*
END CUE: *Darth Vader releases Admiral Motti.*
DURATION: *2 minutes*

Overview: Admiral Motti boasts that the Death Star is the most powerful weapon in the galaxy. Vader warns that no machine can stand before the power of the Force. The Admiral mocks Vader, but he begins to choke, gasping for breath as an invisible hand strangles him. Vader releases Motti, but finds his lack of faith disturbing.

Illustration: Men continue to place their faith in man-made objects instead of in God's power. True, we do not see God in the physical sense, but this should not keep us from placing all of our faith in him alone. Man's creations eventually fail, but the Creator never will.

Questions

- **In today's society, what types of things do people place their faith in?**
- **Do you know people who placed their confidence in something other than God? What happened?**
   Read Psalm 20:7-8.
- **When does having confidence in something other than God become a sin?**
- **What things do you place too much faith in?**
- **How can you increase your faith in God?**

FAITH—Pass the Mustard

Title: THE EMPIRE STRIKES BACK (PG)

Scripture: Matthew 17:18-20

Alternate Take: Miracles (Mark 9:14-27)

START TIME: *1 hour, 8 minutes, 15 seconds*
START CUE: *Luke's X-wing sinks into the swamp.*
END TIME: *1 hour, 10 minutes, 00 seconds*
END CUE: *Yoda says, "My ally is the Force."*
DURATION: *1 minute, 45 seconds*

Overview: Luke's moans that his sunken X-wing will never be recovered. Yoda states that physical size has nothing to do with completing a challenging job. Luke fails to raise his fighter, though, claiming the job is simply too big.

Illustration: In this scene, Luke doesn't even have the faith of a mustard seed. Yoda tells Luke that his lack of faith prevents him from accomplishing great things. God wants to do miraculous things with and through our lives, but we often look at the enormity of a situation and claim the task is impossible. When we realize that God handles the impossible part of a job, it allows him to work miracles through us. (Just once I'd like to levitate the remote control from the TV over to my lazy hand on the couch.)

Questions
- **What is the most miraculous, supernatural thing you have ever seen or experienced?**
- **Has God ever asked you to do something that seemed impossible? What happened?**
  Read Matthew 17:18-20.
- **What does "faith of a mustard seed" mean?**
- **Why does an all-powerful God care if we have faith?**
- **How can your increased faith glorify God in the future?**

FAITH—Use Your Faith, Luke

Title: STAR WARS (PG)

Scripture: Philippians 4:13

Alternate Take: Unbelief (2 Chronicles 36:15-16)

START TIME: *58 minutes, 30 seconds*
START CUE: *Luke practices with his lightsaber.*
END TIME: *1 hour, 00 minutes, 00 seconds*
END CUE: *Obi-Wan congratulates Luke.*
DURATION: *1 minute, 30 seconds*

Overview: Luke practices with his lightsaber against a floating remote. Han Solo claims to trust only in himself, believing that faith in something spiritual is foolish. Luke ignores Han and proves that by trusting in the Force he can do the miraculous—protect himself while he's unable to see.

Illustration: Obviously, this is an analogy and cannot be taken literally since the Force is more New Age than Christian—but that's why this is called an *illustration*. Luke acts by faith, trusting that he will not fail. Get your students talking about how sometimes we must simply do what God asks, even if we're "blindfolded." Obedience increases our faith, and our supernatural success speaks to prebelievers that God is real.

Questions
- **Have people ever responded to your faith in God like that? What happened?**
- **Is following God sometimes like being blindfolded? Why?**
  Read Philippians 4:13.
- **When has God answered your faith in a miraculous or special way? What happened?**
- **How did your faith grow?**
- **What impossible things does God want you to do?**

FAITH—Watch Your Step!

Title: INDIANA JONES AND THE LAST CRUSADE (PG-13)

Scripture: Matthew 14:25-31

Alternate Take: Salvation (Matthew 16:24-26)

START TIME: *1 hour, 47 minutes, 00 seconds*
START CUE: *Indy stands before a chasm.*
END TIME: *1 hour, 48 minutes, 30 seconds*
END CUE: *Indy walks across the "invisible" bridge.*
DURATION: *1 minute, 30 seconds*

Overview: Indy stands at a chasm that separates him from the Holy Grail. He must take an impossible step of faith in order to cross. He does so, stepping out into thin air, and discovers an "invisible" walkway across the chasm.

Illustration: This is literally stepping out in faith. There's not much explanation needed for this one. God constantly asks us to step out into the abyss without a net—in faith—trusting that he will catch us. Though we might be scared to death, God will not let us fall.

Questions

- What is the scariest thing you have ever had to do? What happened?
- What is the scariest thing God has ever asked you to do? Why was it scary?
- Have you ever refused to step out in faith? What happened?
    Read Matthew 14:25-31.
- Why is our faith continually tested?
- How can you step out in faith this week?

FAMILY—Why Can't You Be Like Your Brother?

Title: MR. HOLLAND'S OPUS (PG)

Scripture: Genesis 25:27-28

Alternate Takes: Talents (1 Corinthians 12:4-12), Self-Esteem (Ephesians 2:10)

START TIME: *19 minutes, 45 seconds*
START CUE: *Mr. Holland tells Miss Lang to stop practicing.*
END TIME: *21 minutes, 30 seconds*
END CUE: *Miss Lang leaves.*
DURATION: *1 minute, 45 seconds*

Overview: Miss Lang practices her clarinet, and Mr. Holland tells her to go home. She starts crying because she isn't any good. Mr. Holland encourages her, and Miss Lang reveals that everyone in her family has an amazing talent except her. She just wants to be good at something.

Illustration: Families are a source of joy, comfort...and pressure. Although the comparisons may not be spoken, it's impossible not to compare ourselves to our siblings. Even worse is when we are compared to our siblings by others. Thankfully, God doesn't compare us to anyone in the world. He makes each of us unique and with a different purpose, setting us free from following our family's footsteps so that we may obey God's call.

Questions

- How many of you compare yourselves, or are compared, to a sibling or friend? Why?
- How do the comparisons make you feel?
    Read Genesis 25:27-28.
- How do you think Esau and Jacob felt being compared to each other?
- Why doesn't God compare people?
- How can you help your family stop the comparisons and simply love everyone's differences?

FEAR—'Fraidy Cat

Title: THE TRUMAN SHOW (PG)

Scripture: Isaiah 43:1-3a

Alternate Takes: Faith (John 10:27-29),
Commitment (1 Peter 2:18-19)

START TIME: *6 minutes, 45 seconds*
START CUE: *Truman buys his ticket.*
END TIME: *9 minutes, 00 seconds*
END CUE: *Truman leaves the pier.*
DURATION: *2 minutes, 15 seconds*

Overview: Truman must cross the bay on a ferry to collect an insurance form from a client. He freezes in the middle of the pier, though, unable to get into the boat because of his crippling fear of the water.

Illustration: Fear takes many forms, from simply being afraid of embarrassing yourself to paralyzing phobias like arachibutyrophobia—the fear of peanut butter sticking to the roof of the mouth (that one's too weird to have been made up). Use this clip to start a discussion about how God gives us a life of strength and purpose, not fear, when we place complete trust in him.

Questions
- **What are some phobias people have?**
- **What does fear do to a person's life?**
- **What do you fear?**
     Read Isaiah 43:1-3a.
- **How can you defeat fear in your life?**
- **What other promises from God give you the strength to live free of fear?**

FLIRTING—Who, Me?

Title: RUNAWAY BRIDE (PG)

Scripture: Proverbs 9:13-15

Alternate Takes: Sin Nature (Romans 3:23),
Sin (1 Corinthians 15:34)

START TIME: *42 minutes, 00 seconds*
START CUE: *Peggy enters her hair salon.*
END TIME: *44 minutes, 30 seconds*
END CUE: *Maggie says, "I know."*
DURATION: *2 minutes, 30 seconds*

Overview: Maggie asks if she flirts with Peggy's husband, Cory. Peggy tells her yes, but she knows Maggie can't help it because it's just a natural thing she's always done since childhood. Maggie apologizes for being so screwed up. Peggy tells her everyone is screwed up, but since she knows the flirting hurts people, she should stop.

Illustration: Flirting is a tough issue because it's such a gray area. You can never quite point to something specific and say, "That's wrong," but you still know that it's not right. Flirtation can be harmless, but it often sets up expectations that cannot be fulfilled. Living with integrity in all areas, even when it comes to flirting, is the ideal.

Questions
- **Do you ever flirt with people, even subtly? Why?**
- **Is it a sin to flirt with people?**
  Read Proverbs 9:13-15.
- **Do you think a person who flirts is "loud, undisciplined, and without knowledge"? Why or why not?**
- **When does flirting cross the line, and what message does it send?**
- **How can you avoid flirting in the future?**

FOCUS—Keep Your Eye on the Ball

Title: FORREST GUMP (PG-13)

Scripture: Proverbs 4:25-27

Alternate Take: Commitment (Proverbs 16:3)

START TIME: *58 minutes, 35 seconds*
START CUE: *Forrest is hit on the back of the head by a ping-pong ball.*
END TIME: *59 minutes, 45 seconds*
END CUE: *Forrest plays ping-pong with amazing dexterity.*
DURATION: *1 minute, 15 seconds*

Overview: While recovering from his injuries, Forrest learns how to play ping-pong. His teacher simply instructs him to "keep his eye on the ball." Forrest's uncanny focus on the ping-pong ball makes him a master player.

Illustration: I always knew that I was too smart to be good at ping-pong. (And I guess too smart for football, baseball, hockey…) Focus—that's what it all boils down to. So many things are fighting for our attention, leading us astray. Remaining focused on the Savior, with singular devotion and attention, guarantees a strong finish in this ping-pong life.

Questions
- When were you the most focused on something? What happened?
- What are the top three things you are trying to focus on in your life now?
- What things distract you from those goals?
  Read Proverbs 4:25-27.
- How can you keep your eyes focused on Jesus?
- What distractions do you need to eliminate in order to stay focused on your relationship with Christ?

FOCUS—Who Turned Out the Lights?!

Title: APOLLO 13 (PG)

Scripture: Psalm 78:12-17

Alternate Take: Tragedy (Romans 8:28)

START TIME: *1 hour, 45 minutes*
START CUE: *Jim Lovell is interviewed on TV.*
END TIME: *1 hour, 46 minutes, 30 seconds*
END CUE: *Jim's interview ends.*
DURATION: *1 minute, 30 seconds*

Overview: Jim Lovell, an astronaut, recounts how his fighter plane failed and would crash into the ocean unless he could spot his aircraft carrier. Suddenly, his instruments shorted out, leaving him without lights. The apparent tragedy, however, saved him, since the darkness allowed him to see the ship's wake and follow it to safety.

Illustration: This clip plays like a perfect sermon illustration about focus. Many times we focus on what immediately surrounds us—all of the minor problems and difficulties that take our eyes off of God. Only when we turn our sight completely to God can we clearly see his path and find our way to safety.

Questions
- Have you ever been distracted and missed something important? What happened?
- What things surround you that distract you from God?
- How do distractions affect your life?
  Read Psalm 78:12-17.
- What ways did God use in this Scripture to show his people the right path? What does he do now to guide us?
- What must you do to clear your sight in order to see God's path?

FORGIVENESS—Parents Make Mistakes Too

Title: AUSTIN POWERS: INTERNATIONAL MAN OF MYSTERY (PG-13)

Scripture: Luke 17:3-4

Alternate Takes: Love (John 13:34), Obedience (Ephesians 6:1)

START TIME: *26 minutes, 00 seconds*
START CUE: *Scott meets Dr. Evil.*
END TIME: *27 minutes, 00 seconds*
END CUE: *Scott runs away.*
DURATION: *1 minute*

Overview: Scott Evil meets his father, Dr. Evil, for the first time. Dr. Evil wants a hug from his son, but Scott refuses, saying he hates him because he's never been around.

Illustration: Life involves forgiveness—both giving and receiving. Unfortunately, the family often proves to be the most difficult arena for forgiveness. Due to divorce, lack of communication, workaholism, and neglect, families can have many unresolved conflicts. This silly clip will spark some serious conversation.

Questions
- **Should Scott forgive his dad for being absent?**
- **Does anyone here relate to Scott? How?**
- **Have your parents ever let you down? How?**
    Read Luke 17:3-4.
- **How can God give you a forgiving heart?**
- **How will forgiveness change the everyday relationships in your family?**

THE FUTURE—I Wanna Be a Cowboy

Title: SAY ANYTHING (PG-13)

Scripture: Proverbs 3:5-7

Alternate Take: God's Will (James 4:13-15)

START TIME: *40 minutes, 30 seconds*
START CUE: *Lloyd gets grilled by the dinner guests about his future plans.*
END TIME: *42 minutes, 00 seconds*
END CUE: *Lloyd says, "For now I'm just gonna hang out with your daughter."*
DURATION: *1 minute, 30 seconds*

Overview: Diane's family asks Lloyd "what he's going to do with his life." Lloyd fumblingly details all of the things he will *not* do for a career, ultimately deciding not to worry about it and simply enjoy hanging out with Diane for the summer.

Illustration: The dreaded question looms over most teens: What are you going to do with your life? Thankfully, God has a plan for every person, and faithfully following him gets us to the right place, even when we can't see it. This clip can kick-start a serious, overwhelming, and funny discussion with lots of laughs.

Questions
- **How many of you know what you're going to do in the future? How many don't?**
- **Why is the future so frightening?**
  Read Proverbs 3:5-7.
- **How do these verses challenge you?**
- **What does God say about your future? How does this relate to your career plans?**
- **What is one specific way you'll respond this week to the challenge in Proverbs 3:5-7?**

THE FUTURE—Life Goes On

Title: NEVER BEEN KISSED (PG-13)

Scripture: Colossians 2:6-8

Alternate Takes: Self-Esteem (Psalm 139:13-16), Kindness (1 Thessalonians 5:14-15)

START TIME: *1 hour, 23 minutes, 15 seconds*
START CUE: *The popular girls open up a can of dog food.*
END TIME: *1 hour, 26 minutes, 00 seconds*
END CUE: *Rob runs away.*
DURATION: *2 minutes, 45 seconds*

Overview: Josie prevents the popular kids from pouring dog food on her friend Aldys. After revealing that she's a reporter, Josie tells them that high school doesn't matter in the grand scheme of life. Instead, they should really look at their lives and see what they are building toward.

Illustration: Oscar clip! Oscar clip! Maybe not, but it *does* say everything you've always wanted to tell distraught teens. High school, while traumatic, is only a few years in the many they have on earth. By building toward something in the future, they expand their horizons beyond the school's walls and expand their influence beyond their small circle of friends.

Questions

- How important do you think high school will be to you in ten years? Why?
- What type of future are you building toward? Explain.
  Read Colossians 2:6-8.
- What things should you focus on as you build toward the future?
- How do your actions now affect your future?
- How can you keep a proper perspective on the importance of the present and the future?

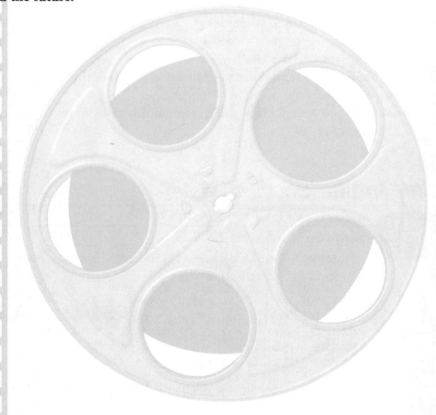

Movie Illustration
THEMES G - K
Generosity...Hypocrisy...Kindness...

GENEROSITY—I Gave at the Office

Title: THE MUPPET CHRISTMAS CAROL (G)

Scripture: Luke 12:32-34

Alternate Take: Greed (Proverbs 21:26)

START TIME: *12 minutes, 00 seconds*
START CUE: *The Professor and Beaker ask Scrooge for money.*
END TIME: *14 minutes, 30 seconds*
END CUE: *The Professor and Beaker leave.*
DURATION: *2 minutes, 30 seconds*

Overview: The Professor and Beaker ask Scrooge to give a contribution to the poor. Scrooge throws them out, saying the poor can live in the prisons.

Illustration: It's no surprise how Scrooge reacts, but it's fun seeing Beaker get harassed. Christians should be charitable, but what we're *supposed* to do and what we *actually* do don't always match. Use this funny gem to introduce a serious topic to your students.

Questions
- **Who do you relate to in the clip? Why?**
- **How do you feel about charities? Why?**
  Read Luke 12:32-34.
- **How are we supposed to live out this passage?**
- **How can you figure out where to use your money?**
- **How and where can you be more generous with your money?**

GOD—Prove Him!

Title: CONTACT (PG)

Scripture: John 20:24-29

Alternate Take: Faith (Matthew 8:5-13)

START TIME: *1 hour, 12 minutes, 45 seconds*
START CUE: *Ellie quizzes Palmer about God.*
END TIME: *1 hour, 15 minutes, 00 seconds*
END CUE: *Palmer tells Ellie to "prove it."*
DURATION: *2 minutes, 15 seconds*

Overview: Ellie debates Palmer about the existence of God. She says that, as a scientist, she needs proof to believe in something. Palmer asks if she loved her deceased father and she says "yes." He asks her to prove it, and Ellie has no response.

Illustration: Burn! (Don't you wish you had a screenwriter crafting all of your comebacks?) Palmer voices a fundamental truth about God—believing in God requires faith. You may not be able to put him in a bottle and prove his existence, but those who seek him *do* find him. God is real for all who choose to see him.

Questions
- **How does God prove his existence to you?**
- **How can you prove his existence to others?**
- **Why doesn't God make himself more visible?**
   Read John 20:24-29.
- **Why is it a greater blessing not to see God?**
- **How can you make God more real to other people?**

GOD'S GLORY—Hitting the Floor

Title: THE WIZARD OF OZ (G)

Scripture: Jude 24–25

Alternate Takes: Fear of God (Jeremiah 10:6-7), Meekness (Ephesians 4:1-2)

START TIME: *1 hour, 9 minutes, 30 seconds*
START CUE: *Dorothy and her friends enter Oz's throne room.*
END TIME: *1 hour, 12 minutes, 30 seconds*
END CUE: *The Cowardly Lion runs out of the throne room.*
DURATION: *3 minutes*

Overview: Dorothy and her friends, trembling and in fear, meet the great Oz. With a floating head, booming voice, and explosions of fire, Oz is a terrible force to behold.

Illustration: It's fun to think about God's throne room. Seeing it will be the most joyful, yet terrifying, experience—beyond our imagination. Oz gives us only a hint of what will happen—standing in humility in the presence of infinite power. We often talk about God as our friend, but it's also good to be reminded of his infinite majesty.

Questions
- **Have you ever been in the presence of someone famous? How did you feel?**
- **How is Oz's throne room like heaven?**
- **How do you feel about standing before God in heaven?**
   Read Jude 24–25.
- **How can God be both personal and awesome?**
- **What are some ways to remind yourself of God's power and majesty this week?**

GOD'S PERSPECTIVE—Seeing the Big Picture

Title: PATCH ADAMS (PG-13)

Scripture: Isaiah 55:8-9

Alternate Takes: Focus (Mark 12:28-31),
Learning (Matthew 11:29),
Listening (Proverbs 1:2-5)

START TIME: *9 minutes, 30 seconds*
START CUE: *Patch asks a question.*
END TIME: *12 minutes, 15 seconds*
END CUE: *Patch leaves the room.*
DURATION: *2 minutes, 45 seconds*

Overview: Patch Adams visits an apparently insane professor to learn the answer to a brainteaser. The professor holds up four fingers and demonstrates that eight fingers appear when you look past yourself to other people. Viewing the world from a different perspective helps you to solve difficult problems.

Illustration: (You, too, can try this trick at home!) We need a new perspective—God's—to answer life's questions and problems. We often come up empty when seeking answers within ourselves. Use this clip to get kids talking about how looking outside themselves to God can open their eyes to new possibilities. God provides clarity and perfect perspective that we can never see from our limited earthly view.

Questions
- **What was the professor's point with the riddle?**
- **How have you found a different perspective while in the middle of a difficult situation? What happened?**
    Read Isaiah 55:8-9.
- **What makes God's perspective better than ours?**
- **Do you always seek God's view on your problems? Why?**
- **How can you learn to make seeking God's perspective your natural response to problems?**

GOD'S PLAN—I'm Special

Title: SIMON BIRCH (PG)

Scripture: Jeremiah 29:11

Alternate Take: Self-Esteem (Psalm 139:13-16)

START TIME: *1 hour, 6 minutes, 45 seconds*
START CUE: *Simon sits in the Rev. Russell's office.*
END TIME: *1 hour, 8 minutes, 15 seconds*

END CUE: *Simon leaves the office.*
DURATION: *1 minute, 30 seconds*

Overview: The Rev. Russell chastises Simon for driving Miss Leavey crazy. Simon tells him that he believes God has a plan for him—that he's God's instrument. He believes God made him small for a reason.

Illustration: God made each of us special. He didn't do that to show off, but because he has a special plan for each of us, whether we believe in him or not. We are his instruments when we allow him to move us the way he desires.

Questions
- **Do you believe God has a plan for your life? What is it?**
- **Do you ever worry about the way people will react to God's plan for your life? Why?**
  Read Jeremiah 29:11.
- **How does this verse make you feel? Why?**
- **Why is a deeper relationship with God important for enjoying his plan?**
- **How can you prepare and be ready when God wants to use you?**

GOD'S PROVISION—I'm the King of the World!

Title: TITANIC (PG-13)

Scripture: Matthew 6:25-34

Alternate Takes: Contentment (1 Timothy 6:6-8), Seize the Day (Proverbs 27:1)

START TIME: *1 hour, 2 minutes, 15 seconds*
START CUE: *Jack describes his life.*
END TIME: *1 hour, 3 minutes, 45 seconds*
END CUE: *Jack raises his glass for a toast.*
DURATION: *1 minute, 30 seconds*

Overview: Jack eats an elaborate dinner with Rose, Cal, and the other wealthy guests on the Titanic. Rose's mother asks Jack how he likes his rootless, unstable existence. Jack says he enjoys taking each day as it comes, making each one count, trusting that somehow his basic needs will be met.

Illustration: Jack echoes God's promise to provide for our needs. (Though the definition of "needs" varies. How cable TV became a utility, I'll never know.) Though we shouldn't emulate Jack's nomadic lifestyle, his peaceful spirit and confidence that his needs will be met can serve as a great discussion-starter about God's provision.

Questions

- **Could you live day to day as Jack does? Why or why not?**
  Read Matthew 6:25-34.
- **How has God provided for your needs?**
- **What is the difference between needs and wants?**
- **What are your actual needs in life?**
- **How can you find contentment in what God has provided for you?**

GOD'S VOICE—Just Do It!

Title: THE SANDLOT (PG)

Scripture: 1 Kings 19:11-13

Alternate Take: Fear (Deuteronomy 31:8)

START TIME: *1 hour, 15 minutes, 00 seconds*
START CUE: *Babe Ruth comes out of Benny's closet.*
END TIME: *1 hour, 17 minutes, 00 seconds*
END CUE: *Babe Ruth takes the Henry Aaron baseball card.*
DURATION: *2 minutes*

Overview: Babe Ruth comes out of Benny's closet to help Benny figure out how to get a lost baseball. Benny says he can't just jump over the fence to get it. Babe tells him that everybody has a chance to do something great, but they're either too scared or don't even recognize the opportunity.

Illustration: If only God would send a celebrity to me every time he wanted me to do something, I would never miss a ministry opportunity. (Yes, sir, Mr. Bond—I will witness to Sam tomorrow.) God has a will for each and every one of us, including some great opportunities to build his kingdom. Many times we are too scared to act or not in a position to hear God when he calls to us. Following God's will requires a faithful heart and attentive ears.

Questions

- **If you could ask anyone in the world to help you with your problems, who would it be? Why?**
  Read 1 Kings 19:11-13.
- **Did Elijah know when God was speaking to him? How do you know when God is speaking to you?**
- **How does knowing God's will help you face difficult situations?**
- **What do you believe is God's will for your life right now? Why?**
- **What can you do to enable yourself to hear God's will for your life?**

GOD'S WILL—Don't Wimp Out!

Title: STAR WARS (PG)

Scripture: Judges 6:14-17

Alternate Takes: Helping Others (Matthew 5:42),
Faith (Romans 12:3)

START TIME: *34 minutes, 30 seconds*
START CUE: *Princess Leia's message begins.*
END TIME: *36 minutes, 30 seconds*
END CUE: *Obi-Wan concedes to Luke.*
DURATION: *2 minutes*

Overview: Luke and Obi-Wan listen to Princess Leia's desperate plea for help in defeating the Empire. Obi-Wan invites Luke to help him rescue the princess, but Luke refuses, claiming the mission is too crazy and too far away. Obi-Wan counters that Luke speaks his uncle's words and not his own.

Illustration: God just doesn't get it. When God asks us to do something, it should be a simple, convenient task. Instead, he always asks the impossible, stretching our faith and risking our comfort! That's why we refuse, defer, or cower in fear instead of leaping into action. Often we've got too much of cautious Luke in us when God calls and not enough bold faith.

Questions
- **What were the real reasons Luke refused to help Obi-Wan?**
  Read Judges 6:14-17.
- **How do you feel about Gideon's response?**
- **Why do we sometimes hesitate when God calls?**
- **Why does following God involve risk?**
- **What is God asking you to risk in your life to serve him, and how will you respond to his call?**

GOD'S WILL—It Was in the Stars

Title: CAN'T HARDLY WAIT (PG-13)

Scripture: 1 Peter 4:1-2

Alternate Take: Love (1 Corinthians 13)

START TIME: *3 minutes, 45 seconds*
START CUE: *Preston recounts how he and Amanda are connected.*
END TIME: *5 minutes, 30 seconds*
END CUE: *Preston believes that fate has given him a second chance.*
DURATION: *1 minute, 45 seconds*

Themes G-K

Overview: Preston relives the first moment he saw Amanda and all of the coincidental circumstances that lead him to believe that they are destined to be together. Now that she is single, he's not going to miss this opportunity to be with her.

Illustration: If she picks up the phone on the third ring, then that means we're supposed to go out. (Come on, *everybody* thinks silly stuff like that...don't they?) People place WAY too much stock in fate and read into every coincidence exactly what they want to see. God doesn't deal in coincidences, though, just his plan. By seeking him in everything, the differences between fate and his desires come to light.

Questions
- **What is the most eerie coincidence you can remember, and what did you think it meant?**
- **Do you believe in fate?**
    Read 1 Peter 4:1-2.
- **How does your view of fate relate to this passage and "the will of God"?**
- **How can you distinguish between your own confidence and God's will?**
- **What evil desires in your life must you stop working for?**

GOD'S WILL—What Does He Really Want?

Title: SIMON BIRCH (PG)

Scripture: 1 Samuel 15:22

Alternate Takes: Confrontation (Matthew 18:15), Reverence (Leviticus 19:30)

START TIME: *28 minutes, 00 seconds*
START CUE: *The Rev. Russell concludes his sermon.*
END TIME: *29 minutes, 45 seconds*
END CUE: *He excuses the kids to go to Sunday school.*
DURATION: *1 minute, 45 seconds*

Overview: The Rev. Russell asks everyone to listen to the church announcements. Simon Birch moans, saying that God doesn't care about the announcements. Russell asks what's wrong, and Simon stands up in church and says that God doesn't care if they have a continental breakfast or not.

Illustration: I wonder how many things we do for God that he never asked of us or wanted in the first place. Instead of blindly doing stuff, we should ask ourselves what God really wants. If we did, we'd probably learn he wants fewer works and more people living like his Son.

Questions

- **What types of things do Christians do for God that aren't really for God after all?**
- **What are the truly important things we do as a church?**
- **How do you determine what are the important things and what are just extras?**
    Read 1 Samuel 15:22.
- **In your personal life, what things do you focus a lot of energy on that aren't really very important? Why?**
- **What will you do this week to focus on what is really important to God?**

GOSSIP—Did You Hear?

Title: YOU'VE GOT MAIL (PG)

Scripture: Proverbs 20:19

Alternate Take: Standing Firm (2 Thessalonians 2:15)

START TIME: *1 hour, 9 minutes, 15 seconds*
START CUE: *Kathleen opens the bookstore.*
END TIME: *1 hour, 11 minutes, 15 seconds*
END CUE: *Kathleen says, "That was different."*
DURATION: *2 minutes*

Overview: Kathleen and Christina wonder why Kathleen's date stood her up. They propose various scenarios until George comes into the shop with a newspaper article about a rapist being captured. They decide that her date was the rapist and that Kathleen escaped a horrible fate.

Illustration: Did you hear about…? The buck has to stop somewhere, so it might as well be with Christians. Too much time and energy goes into talking and guessing about other people. Gossip kills reputations and destroys friendships, when friendships could be saved by simply asking someone the truth. This extreme example can get your kids digging deep into an issue we've all faced: the temptation to gossip.

Questions

- **What's the most recent rumor you've heard?**
- **Did you find out from the person involved if it was true? Why or why not?**
    Read Proverbs 20:19.
- **What negative things happen because of gossip?**
- **How can Christians respond to gossip in a Christlike way?**
- **How can you avoid situations this week where you would normally participate in gossip?**

(sidebar) **Themes G–K**

GREED—I've Almost Got It...

Title: INDIANA JONES AND THE LAST CRUSADE (PG-13)

Scripture: 1 Timothy 6:9-11

Alternate Take: Obedience (Jeremiah 42:6)

START TIME: *1 hour, 56 minutes, 30 seconds*
START CUE: *Indy catches Elsa by the wrist.*
END TIME: *1 hour, 57 minutes, 45 seconds*
END CUE: *Indy grabs his dad with both hands.*
DURATION: *1 minute, 15 seconds*

Overview: Indy saves Elsa from falling into a chasm. Elsa reaches for the Grail instead of Indy's hand, and she ultimately slips out of his grasp into the abyss. Suddenly Indy lands in the same situation, with his dad begging him to give up the Grail and grab his hand. Indy does, giving up the Grail and saving himself.

Illustration: Greed consumes people. They make rash and dangerous decisions in their quest for more things. Temporal pleasures and wealth never satisfy people and can eventually drag them down. This world is only a blip on the radar screen of eternity, so cling to God, not to possessions.

Questions
- **What are some things your friends are greedy for? What about the adults you know?**
- **Are these people ever satisfied? Why or why not?**
  Read 1 Timothy 6:9-11.
- **How can you overcome greed in your life?**
- **What things do you need to stop reaching for?**
- **How can you grab on to God with both hands this week?**

GUILT—Oh, the Shame!

Title: THE LION KING (G)

Scripture: John 4:7-18

Alternate Takes: Satan (Revelation 12:10),
Forgiveness (John 8:3-11),
Confession (James 5:16)

START TIME: *1 hour, 14 minutes, 00 seconds*
START CUE: *Simba confronts Scar.*
END TIME: *1 hour, 16 minutes, 15 seconds*
END CUE: *Simba leaps on top of Scar.*
DURATION: *2 minutes, 15 seconds*

Overview: Simba returns to reclaim the throne from his uncle, Scar. Scar, however, brings up Simba's past mistake—being responsible for his father Mufasa's death. Scar insinuates that Simba's guilty past disqualifies him from doing right in the present. Simba's guilt throws him into doubt and nearly kills him, until Scar admits that he was the one who killed Mufasa.

Illustration: Satan knows guilt. He can twist and manipulate past failures to stop us from doing God's will in the present. He loves it when we pull ourselves out of the race because of guilt. Guilt disables us; but experiencing God's forgiveness (and forgiving ourselves) allows us to move forward and be used by God. Use this scene to kick off a discussion about tackling the power of guilt and shame.

Questions
- **Why is guilt so powerful?**
  Read John 4:7-18.
- **How do you think the Samaritan woman felt when Jesus confronted her about her lifestyle?**
- **Have you ever felt guilty about something? How did you deal with it?**
- **God forgives you, but how do you forgive *yourself* for mistakes?**
- **Do you need to release any guilt in your life? What's stopping you?**

GUILT–Sleepless Nights

Title: RAISING ARIZONA (PG-13)

Scripture: Hosea 5:15

Alternate Take: Dreams (Job 33:14-18)

START TIME: *27 minutes, 30 seconds*
START CUE: *Hi has a nightmare.*
END TIME: *29 minutes, 00 seconds*
END CUE: *Hi wakes up.*
DURATION: *1 minute, 30 seconds*

Overview: The Rider of the Apocalypse comes to Hi in a nightmare. Hi, wracked with guilt over his part in kidnapping Nathan, Jr., witnesses the cruelty of the Rider as he burns across the country on his motorcycle from hell.

Illustration: I wish my dreams were this funny. This surreal, over-the-top scene shows how guilt can take over our minds. Even when we get away with something, the guilt doesn't leave us alone, even when we sleep. The only way to defeat guilt is to seek forgiveness.

Questions
- **Have you ever had a crazy dream like that? What was it?**

- **What are some of the reasons we dream certain things?**
    Read Hosea 5:15.
- **According to this verse, what is God's perspective on guilt?**
- **How do guilty feelings affect you?**
- **How do you need to deal with guilty feelings?**

HEAVEN—All This and More!

Title: WAKING NED DEVINE (PG)

Scripture: Revelation 21:10-24

Alternate Take: Salvation (Titus 3:3-7)

START TIME: *50 minutes, 30 seconds*
START CUE: *Michael says, "Oh, yes, the ticket."*
END TIME: *52 minutes, 00 seconds*
END CUE: *Jim says, "Right, let's have a look."*
DURATION: *1 minute, 30 seconds*

Overview: Michael (pretending to be Ned) presents his winning lottery ticket to Jim, who tells him the astounding amount of money that he has won. The number is so far beyond his dreams that Michael can only stammer and make noises.

Illustration: This is what heaven will be like! We'll stand at the gates and be stunned at how far beyond our limited comprehension the reality of heaven is. Heaven is where we're headed for eternity, so use this clip to take a few moments with your students to dream about this wondrous place.

Questions
- **What do you think heaven will be like?**
- **What do you think you'll be doing in heaven?**
    Read Revelation 21:10-24.
- **How does this description strike you? Why do you think the Bible doesn't have a completely clear description of heaven?**
- **What do you imagine seeing God will be like?**
- **How does the reality of heaven affect your everyday life?**

HELPING OTHERS—The Bad Samaritan

Title: AUSTIN POWERS: THE SPY WHO SHAGGED ME (PG-13)

Scripture: Luke 10:30-37

Alternate Take: Generosity (Matthew 5:40-44)

START TIME: *34 minutes, 15 seconds*
START CUE: *Austin looks over the edge of the cliff.*
END TIME: *34 minutes, 45 seconds*
END CUE: *Austin walks away from the cliff.*
DURATION: *30 seconds*

Overview: Dr. Evil's henchman, Mustafa, is injured at the bottom of a ravine. He cries out to Austin Powers for help, but Austin ignores him, leaving him to suffer.

Illustration: This ultrabrief scene presents an absurd update of the popular parable. Though we would never leave someone lying at the bottom of a ravine, we do pass by needy people every day. Use this exaggerated example to help your students evaluate their own reactions to people in need.

Questions
- **Should Austin have helped Mustafa?**
- **Have you ever walked away from someone who needed help? Why?**
- **What are some common reasons for not stopping to help people?**
  Read Luke 10:30-37.
- **Who do you have contact with who needs help?**
- **What are practical ways you can help needy people every day?**

Themes G-K

HELPING OTHERS—Well Excuuuuse Me!

Title: THE MUPPET MOVIE (G)

Scripture: Mark 10:43-45

Alternate Takes: Flattery (Proverbs 29:5), Mockery (Proverbs 14:6-7)

START TIME: *49 minutes, 45 seconds*
START CUE: *The waiter comes to "serve" Kermit and Miss Piggy.*
END TIME: *51 minutes, 30 seconds*
END CUE: *The waiter leaves, bowing, saying "Thank you, thank you."*
DURATION: *1 minute, 45 seconds*

Overview: Steve Martin is the worst waiter in history, giving sarcastic service to Kermit and Miss Piggy on their date.

Illustration: Service like this typically earns someone a first-class ticket to unemployment. The attitude, though, is commonplace. Today, being a servant is looked down upon, with people continually asserting their so-called rights and their station in life. This scene shows how ridiculous rejecting a servant attitude becomes.

Questions

- Have you ever encountered someone this rude? What happened?
- Why is it hard to serve people, even when it's your job?
  Read Mark 10:43-45.
- What messages does the world send that run counter to having a servant's heart?
- How do people react to you when you serve them?
- How can you become a better servant this week?

HELPING OTHERS—Answering the Call

Title: THE LION KING (G)

Scripture: James 2:15-16

Alternate Take: Selfishness (Philippians 2:21)

START TIME: *1 hour, 00 minutes, 30 seconds*
START CUE: *Simba and Rafiki walk and talk.*
END TIME: *1 hour, 2 minutes, 00 seconds*
END CUE: *Simba and Rafiki finish fighting.*
DURATION: *1 minute, 30 seconds*

Overview: Rafiki wants Simba to return home and help to free the lions from the rule of Simba's evil uncle, Scar. Simba refuses, claiming that it's no concern of his. He lives a carefree, "hakuna matata" lifestyle, worrying only about himself. Rafiki disagrees. He believes Simba cannot turn a blind eye to the suffering of others, because every life affects others.

Illustration: "It's all about ME!" That's why we have so many lawsuits and so many slackers today. "As long as I don't bother anyone, they have no right to bother me"—what a crock! Scripture declares that we *must* care for others. (Sorry, it's not just a request.) We cannot cut ourselves off from the world and from the needs of others, because we're all in this together whether we like it or not.

Questions

- Was Simba right to think that the problems back home were not his problems? Why or why not?
- What effects can an attitude like Simba's have on the world?
  Read James 2:15-16.
- How does helping others affect the world?
- Why does God call us to help other people?
- What specific problem has God opened your eyes to that you can help someone with?

HELPING OTHERS—I Can Help!

Title: STAR WARS: EPISODE 1—
THE PHANTOM MENACE (PG)

Scripture: Matthew 25:34-40

Alternate Take: Seeking Help (Matthew 7:7-11)

START TIME: *42 minutes, 15 seconds*
START CUE: *Qui-Gon says, "I can see there's no fooling you."*
END TIME: *44 minutes, 00 seconds*
END CUE: *Shmi says, "He can help you."*
DURATION: *1 minute, 45 seconds*

Overview: Qui-Gon admits to Anakin and Anakin's mother Shmi that they need to raise money to buy parts for the ship. Anakin offers to enter the pod race and win the money. Shmi doesn't like the idea, but agrees to allow Anakin to do it after he says, "You always say the big problem in the universe is no one helps each other."

Illustration: Way to go, Anakin! (Too bad you become pure evil.) The big problem in the *Star Wars* universe holds true in our galaxy as well. Cry out for help and hear your voice echo for miles! Use this illustration to help your students explore why Jesus calls us to help one another, even our enemies, in times of need—no questions asked.

Questions
• **Has a stranger ever bailed you out? What happened?**
• **Why is it rare for people to help strangers today?**
  Read Matthew 25:34-40.
• **Do you feel convicted by these verses? Why?**
• **How can you make yourself more aware of the needs of others?**
• **Who is someone you can help this week without their knowing it? What will you do?**

HONESTY—Yeah, That's the Ticket!

Title: ALADDIN (G)

Scripture: Psalm 15

Alternate Takes: Appearances (1 Samuel 16:7),
Dating (Ephesians 4:25),
Contentment (Ephesians 2:10)

START TIME: *54 minutes, 00 seconds*
START CUE: *Aladdin's friends try to convince him to tell the truth.*

END TIME: *54 minutes, 45 seconds*
END CUE: *Aladdin leaves on the flying carpet.*
DURATION: *45 seconds*

Overview: Aladdin's friends encourage him to 'fess up that he's a street urchin and not the prince he pretends to be. Aladdin, worried that Princess Jasmine won't like him, decides to continue his charade and win Princess Jasmine's heart.

Illustration: Driving a station wagon throughout high school eliminated any question of girls dating *me* for status! In a status-obsessed society, the desire to lie about ourselves happens fairly often. Honesty about who we are, though, is always the best policy.

Questions
- **What is the biggest lie someone has told you about themselves?**
- **What lies have you told other people about yourself? What happened?**
- **Why weren't you honest?**
  Read Psalm 15.
- **What are the benefits of living honestly? How would choosing to live honestly change the world?**
- **How do you need to grow to live in honesty about yourself?**

HYPOCRISY—Every Day is Halloween

Title: THE MASK (PG-13)

Scripture: Matthew 15:7-9

Alternate Takes: Contentment (Ephesians 2:10), Integrity (Psalm 25:21)

START TIME: *16 minutes, 45 seconds*
START CUE: *Stanley watches a TV program about "masks."*
END TIME: *18 minutes, 15 seconds*
END CUE: *Stanley picks up the mask.*
DURATION: *1 minute, 30 seconds*

Overview: Stanley Ipkiss watches a TV interview of a professor who explains that all people wear "masks" in order to hide their true selves. Stanley tries on his newfound wooden mask and dramatically morphs into his bizarre alter ego who boldly acts out all of Stanley's secret desires.

Illustration: Christ calls us to be open and genuine with each other because living transparent, honest lives helps lead others to the transforming love of Christ. Unfortunately, many Christians hide behind masks—typically a mask of perfection. (Of course, that would be everyone else, not you.) Wearing a mask, though, only hinders the work God wants to do in you and through you. Use this silly clip to help students dig deeper into the issue of hypocrisy.

Questions
- **What types of masks do people wear?**
- **What happens when we wear masks?**
    Read Matthew 15:7-9.
- **Why does Jesus call the Pharisees hypocrites? Does this relate to people today?**
- **How does this passage challenge you personally?**
- **What "mask" do you need to remove from your life?**

IDOLS—I Wanna Be Like Mike!

Title: FORREST GUMP (PG-13)

Scripture: 1 Corinthians 10:12-14

Alternate Take: Faith (Joshua 24:15)

START TIME: *1 hour, 57 minutes, 15 seconds*
START CUE: *Forrest and his followers run through the desert.*
END TIME: *1 hour, 58 minutes, 45 seconds*
END CUE: *Forrest leaves his followers alone in the desert.*
DURATION: *1 minute, 30 seconds*

Overview: Forrest stops running and his followers stop, waiting to hear what he has to say. Forrest simply says, "I wanna go home." He leaves his followers stranded in the middle of the desert, with no one to lead them.

Illustration: We may not worship little gold and wooden idols, but we still have our own modern idols (like TV sets and VCRs, perhaps?—ironic, I know, coming from a guy who watches tons of movies). Around the world, people follow their favorite singers, movie stars, athletes, pastors, or others, and they end up disappointed, disillusioned, and standing in the desert without a leader. God hates idols because they steal his adoration and they ultimately hurt us.

Questions
- **Who have you looked up to and been disappointed by? What happened?**
- **Who and what are some of our idols in the world today? Why do you think God hates idols so much?**
    Read 1 Corinthians 10:12-14.
- **Why is idolatry such a common temptation? How do you feel tempted by it?**
- **How can you determine if something is an idol in your life?**
- **What idols do you need to flee from? How will you flee?**

INTEGRITY—Obeying God Foremost

Title: REBEL WITHOUT A CAUSE (Not Rated)

Scripture: Acts 5:27-32

Alternate Take: Truth (John 8:32)

START TIME: *1 hour, 1 minute, 00 seconds*
START CUE: *Jim confesses to his parents.*
END TIME: *1 hour, 3 minutes, 30 seconds*
END CUE: *Jim leaves the house.*
DURATION: *2 minutes, 30 seconds*

Overview: Jim wants to tell the police the truth about a tragedy he was involved in, but his parents forbid him to. They argue about truth and doing the right thing. Jim's parents end the dispute with a "do as I say, not as I do" defense.

Illustration: Modern-day truth is a tricky thing. Half-truths and outright lies often win out, especially when mixed with messages from parents, teachers, and peers. Sometimes an authority figure may tell you to do something that contradicts God's Word. The trick is to figure out how to honor that person and still obey God. This clip will get kids talking about the importance of obeying God above all else.

Questions
- **What do you relate to in this scene?**
- **How would you have reacted in Jim's situation?**
- **Has anyone ever asked you to disobey God? What happened?**
  Read Acts 5:27-32.
- **Is it possible to honor an ungodly authority and obey God at the same time? How?**
- **Are there situations in your life where you'll need to obey God instead of man? What will you do?**

INTEGRITY—Standing by Your Word

Title: THE OUTLAW JOSEY WALES (PG)

Scripture: James 5:12

Alternate Takes: Peace (Romans 14:19), Oaths (Numbers 30:2)

START TIME: *1 hour, 49 minutes, 15 seconds*
START CUE: *Josey and Ten Bears meet.*
END TIME: *1 hour, 51 minutes, 30 seconds*

END CUE: *Josey and Ten Bears agree.*
DURATION: *2 minutes, 15 seconds*

Overview: Josey Wales meets Ten Bears, the American Indian chief in control of the region in which Josey and his friends want to settle. Josey wants to live in peace with Ten Bears and guarantees that his word is honorable. Ten Bears believes Josey and laments the fact that few men keep their word.

Illustration: Promises are cheap today. (Unless Clint Eastwood is making the promise!) God's command to "let your 'yes' be yes" is illustrated in this scene. This is a glaring reminder when applied to American Indians, whose harsh life today stems directly from past broken promises. God, who embodies honesty and integrity, calls us to conform to his image. It's easier said than done, but God deserves nothing less.

Questions
• **Why did Ten Bears accept Josey's word?**
• **Do you accept people at their word today? Why or why not?**
• **What is integrity, and how do you see it in life?**
    Read James 5:12.
• **Is this type of integrity common in our society? Why or why not?**
• **How can you build integrity into your life?**

INTEGRITY—This Is Your Life

Title: THE TRUMAN SHOW (PG)

Scripture: Psalm 69:5

Alternate Take: Omniscience (1 John 3:18-20)

START TIME: *1 hour, 1 minute, 15 seconds*
START CUE: *The montage of Truman's life begins.*
END TIME: *1 hour, 2 minutes, 00 seconds*
END CUE: *The montage of Truman's life ends.*
DURATION: *45 seconds*

Overview: A Truman Burbank montage reveals that a satellite has transmitted images of his life worldwide, 24 hours a day, 7 days a week, 365 days a year since the day he was born.

Illustration: Though we don't know exactly how Judgment Day will play out, we do know that God sees how we live every moment of our lives. This knowledge should spur us to live every moment in devotion to him.

Themes G-K

Questions

- **What would be the worst part about having your daily life broadcast on TV?**
- **How would you live differently if your life was broadcast like Truman's?**
  Read Psalm 69:5.
- **How does it feel to know that God is always watching you? Does it feel comforting or convicting? Why?**
- **Does God's watching you 24/7 affect how you live your life? Explain.**
- **How will you change some of the embarrassing "hidden" things in your life?**

INTEGRITY—You Can't Buy Me

Title: THE MUPPET MOVIE (G)

Scripture: Acts 8:18-23

Alternate Take: Greed (Matthew 23:25)

START TIME: *23 minutes, 45 seconds*
START CUE: *Hopper talks to Kermit and Fozzie in the car.*
END TIME: *25 minutes, 00 seconds*
END CUE: *Max opens the car door for Hopper.*
DURATION: *1 minute, 15 seconds*

Overview: Doc Hopper begs Kermit the Frog to become the spokesman for his chain of frog-leg restaurants. Kermit refuses to take part, no matter how much money Hopper offers him. Hopper's assistant agrees with Kermit, and he quits right then and there on moral grounds—but he immediately rejoins Hopper when he's given a pay raise.

Illustration: You gotta love America! So many people will fight tooth and nail for a cause...until they're offered lots of cash to change their mind. Kermit and Max represent the two extremes of integrity. Kermit rejects compromise, while Max quickly sells his morals. We can all learn a bit from our green friend! Use Kermit's example to start a discussion about how Christians should stand in integrity on God's Word and never waver.

Questions

- **Do you know people who have integrity? How do they exhibit integrity to you?**
  Read Acts 8:18-23.
- **How else could Peter have responded to Simon's offer? What would have happened if he had accepted the money?**
- **Can money destroy a person's integrity? How?**

- Can *your* values be bought? Why or why not?
- How can you build integrity into your life?

INTEGRITY—You Find a Million Dollars...

Title: EDWARD SCISSORHANDS (PG-13)

Scripture: 2 Corinthians 7:1-2

Alternate Take: Parents (Ephesians 6:4)

START TIME: *1 hour, 11 minutes, 45 seconds*
START CUE: *Dad gives Edward a hypothetical moral dilemma.*
END TIME: *1 hour, 13 minutes, 30 seconds*
END CUE: *Dad finishes teaching Edward about right and wrong.*
DURATION: *1 minute, 45 seconds*

Overview: Dad asks Edward a question: If you found a case full of money, what would you do? Edward would give the money to his family, but Dad tells him he must give the money to the police. Edward has difficulty understanding that the nice thing is not always the right thing.

Illustration: We often make decisions by the seat of our pants based on circumstances and feelings. Sometimes what appears to be right is not right. God's Word provides a guide for building integrity and helps us develop an understanding that God's answers are always right.

Questions
- Do you agree with Edward or his dad? Why?
- What is the worst moral dilemma you have been in? What happened?
- How do you make decisions in moral dilemmas?
    Read 2 Corinthians 7:1-2.
- What do these verses have to do with integrity?
- How does living a life of integrity help you with choices in your life?

INTEGRITY—You Saw Me?

Title: GALAXY QUEST (PG)

Scripture: 1 Peter 2:21-22

Alternate Take: Helping Others (1 John 3:16-18)

START TIME: *25 minutes, 45 seconds*
START CUE: *The Thermians show the Galaxy Quest cast their ship.*
END TIME: *27 minutes, 30 seconds*

Themes G-K

END CUE: *The Galaxy Quest crew members chicken out.*
DURATION: *1 minute, 45 seconds*

Overview: The Thermians have watched the *Galaxy Quest* crew's adventures from their planet light-years away. (They believe that the canceled TV series is actual history.) They tell the crew that they need their help in fighting General Sarris, who seeks their extermination.

Illustration: You never know when someone is watching you. We represent Christ here on earth (Jesus in the flesh) to people who do not know him. We often have no idea when people are watching us and how our actions affect them. This illustration can get kids talking about the importance of living by Christ's high standards so that everyone who watches our lives will be drawn to Jesus.

Questions
- **Have you ever been disappointed by someone's actions when that person didn't know you were watching? What happened?**
  Read 1 Peter 2:21-22.
- **How are you following Christ's example?**
- **How do your actions reflect upon Jesus?**
- **Is there something you are involved in or an attitude you have that would be embarrassing for someone to see?**
- **How can you rid your life of un-Christlike actions and attitudes?**

JUDGING—Just Look at Her!

Title: MONTY PYTHON AND THE HOLY GRAIL (PG)
Scripture: Matthew 11:17-19
Alternate Takes: Gossip (Leviticus 19:16), Persecution (Acts 13:50)

START TIME: *17 minutes, 30 seconds*
START CUE: *The people drag a "witch" before Sir Bedevere.*
END TIME: *20 minutes, 15 seconds*
END CUE: *The people drag the woman away.*
DURATION: *2 minutes, 45 seconds*

Overview: A mob drags a woman before Sir Bedevere and claims the woman is a witch. Sir Bedevere questions their evidence, and they confess they made it all up—but they want to burn the woman as a witch nonetheless.

Illustration: We may not judge people as witches anymore, but we judge them by everything else under the sun—including their clothing, job, friends, music, and family. (How often do people immediately assume things about you once they categorize you as a Christian?) Humanity loves jumping to conclusions about others. Yet God calls us to treat every person the same, no matter what we've seen or heard.

Questions
- **What are some ways we judge people today?**
- **Have you ever jumped to the wrong conclusions about someone? What happened?**
    Read Matthew 11:17-19.
- **How did people judge Jesus and John the Baptist? Why do you think they labeled Jesus and John that way?**
- **How are Christians supposed to respond to people's appearances and actions? Why is it hard sometimes?**
- **How can you train yourself not to judge others?**

KINDNESS—Show a Little Tenderness

Title: BEAUTY AND THE BEAST (G)

Scripture: 1 Thessalonians 5:14-15

Alternate Takes: Angels (Hebrews 13:2), Appearances (John 7:24)

START TIME: *45 seconds*
START CUE: *The storybook opens.*
END TIME: *2 minutes, 45 seconds*
END CUE: *The prince becomes the Beast.*
DURATION: *2 minutes*

Overview: A young prince turns away an old beggar woman in a storm and refuses to help her. The beggar turns into a beautiful enchantress who transforms the young prince into a hideous beast because of his cruelty. The spell will only be broken when he learns to love others.

Illustration: There would be many "Beasts" running around if God punished all cruelty this way! Kindness is free to give, but is not often given freely. This illustration can get kids talking about how God calls us to demonstrate his love by helping anyone who asks.

Questions
- **What is the meanest thing you have ever seen someone do?**
- **Why do some people refuse to be kind to others?**

- Are Christians known for their kindness at your school? in society at large? Why or why not?

  Read 1 Thessalonians 5:14-15.
- What are simple ways you can show kindness to other people, even to strangers?
- How can we join together and show kindness in our community?

Movie Illustration
THEMES L - Q
Loneliness...Materialism...Purpose...

LONELINESS—Does Anybody See Me?

Title: CAN'T HARDLY WAIT (PG-13)

Scripture: Acts 2:46-47

Alternate Take: Reaching Out (1 John 3:17-18)

START TIME: *28 minutes, 00 seconds*
START CUE: *Denise sits by herself.*
END TIME: *28 minutes, 45 seconds*
END CUE: *The kids pay up on their bet.*
DURATION: *45 seconds*

Overview: Denise sits by herself in the middle of a huge party. Finally, a girl sits beside her and asks her if they had been in language lab together. Denise says yes and the girl tells her friends, "I told you she went to our school!"

Illustration: It's an amazing fact that a person can feel completely alone in a room full of people. (Living in Los Angeles, I see it every day.) This situation is funny in a film, but not when played out in real life. Everyone longs for relationships, and a church family is exactly where they should find them.

Questions
- **When have you felt lonely?**
- **How can someone feel lonely in a room full of people?**
- **Why should loneliness never enter the church?**
  Read Acts 2:46-47.
- **How would you describe the relationships in the early church? Do you think people felt lonely? Why or why not?**
- **How can we make sure no one who comes to this group ever feels lonely?**

LONELINESS—Wanted: A Friend

Title: REAR WINDOW (PG)

Scripture: Psalm 25:15-21

Alternate Take: Reaching Out (James 4:17)

START TIME: *21 minutes, 00 seconds*
START CUE: *Jeff watches Miss Lonelyheart.*
END TIME: *23 minutes, 15 seconds*
END CUE: *Miss Lonelyheart cries.*
DURATION: *2 minutes, 15 seconds*

Overview: Jeff watches Miss Lonelyheart pretend that she has a gentleman eating dinner with her—pretending to open the door, sit, and eat dinner with the man. Miss Lonelyheart finally breaks down and cries in her desperate loneliness.

Illustration: Cities grow larger and people grow lonelier. Even in church, people long for meaningful friendships with others. After all, we all feel lonely sometimes! Though we can find relief from loneliness through relationships with other Christians, ultimately we must find our hope in Jesus.

Questions
- **Have you ever felt overwhelmingly lonely? When?**
- **What types of situations lead people to feel this lonely?**
- **How do you deal with loneliness? What helps?**
  Read Psalm 25:15-21.
- **What was David's solution for his loneliness?**
- **How can we deal with loneliness in our group?**

LOVE—Goin' to the Chapel

Title: FERRIS BUELLER'S DAY OFF (PG-13)

Scripture: Genesis 2:22-24

Alternate Take: Divorce (Proverbs 5:15-20)

START TIME: *39 minutes, 45 seconds*
START CUE: *Ferris proposes to Simone.*
END TIME: *40 minutes, 30 seconds*
END CUE: *Cameron makes a "drip" sound with his mouth.*
DURATION: *45 seconds*

Overview: Ferris impulsively proposes to Simone, claiming that (even though they're both teenagers) there's no reason they shouldn't get hitched. Cameron disagrees, pointing to his parents and how much they hate each other.

Illustration: Though much of society might think this scene is great, sane minds understand that marriage is a huge commitment. The current divorce trend skews the perspective on the institution and the nature of love itself. True love is not flighty and lightning quick, but instead it is developed through sacrifice and service.

Questions
- **Do you think Ferris and Simone would have a good marriage? Why or why not?**
- **Why do people take marriage lightly?**
- **What creates a love that lasts?**
  Read Genesis 2:22-24.
- **What is the most important part of a marriage?**
- **What qualities will you look for in a person you want to marry?**

LOVE—Go On Without Me

Title: FORREST GUMP (PG-13)

Scripture: John 15:13

Alternate Take: Dealing With Death (Galatians 3:29)

START TIME: *50 minutes, 45 seconds*
START CUE: *Forrest sprints away from the fighting.*
END TIME: *52 minutes, 15 seconds*
END CUE: *Forrest saves members of his platoon. (Stop before Forrest finds Lt. Dan.)*
DURATION: *1 minute, 30 seconds*

Overview: Forrest retreats from a gunfight. Realizing he is all alone, he returns to the battlefield and risks his life to find wounded comrades and carry them to safety.

Illustration: Few of us truly understand the horrors of war (watching *Saving Private Ryan* twenty times doesn't count). Physically laying down our lives for someone is not an ever-present reality. We can demonstrate a servant's heart, though—proving our love toward others by continually laying our lives at their feet. This moving example of self-sacrifice can prompt students to consider Jesus' sacrificial love.

Questions
- **Do you think you would have done what Forrest did? How would you have felt?**
- **What is the most loving, sacrificial thing someone has ever done for you? What have you done for another?**
- **Is it in our nature to sacrifice for others? Why or why not?**
  Read John 15:13.
- **Who do you consider to be your friends? Who does God consider friends?**
- **In what ways can you lay down your life for other people in your everyday life?**

LUST—Look, Don't Touch

Title: THE MASK (PG-13)

Scripture: Matthew 5:27-28

Alternate Takes: Modesty (1 Timothy 2:9-10), Temptation (1 Corinthians 6:18)

START TIME: *3 minutes, 30 seconds*
START CUE: *Tina enters the bank.*
END TIME: *4 minutes, 30 seconds*
END CUE: *Tina sits at Stanley's desk.*
DURATION: *1 minute*

Overview: Stanley Ipkiss and his co-worker ogle Tina Carlyle as she enters the bank. Their eyes practically fall out of their heads as Tina walks across the lobby (in slo-mo), and they obviously display the lust in their hearts.

Illustration: God is very explicit about his feelings toward lust—he hates it. Lust, however, is rampant today in the media and evident in loose social mores. God's people must awaken to this fact and be encouraged to combat lust in all of its forms. Use this clip to kick-start a discussion on this critical topic.

Questions
- **What sins do you see in this scene?**
  Read Matthew 5:27-28.
- **Why does God hate lust so much?**
- **Where does lust eventually lead?**
- **What should Stanley have done to avoid lust?**
- **How can you avoid lust in all areas of your life?**

LYING—It's Still Growing!

Title: ALADDIN (G)

Scripture: Colossians 3:9-10

Alternate Takes: Integrity (James 5:12), Trust (Psalm 33:18-22)

START TIME: *1 hour, 7 minutes, 00 seconds*
START CUE: *The Genie talks about his plans for freedom.*
END TIME: *1 hour, 8 minutes, 30 seconds*
END CUE: *The Genie goes back into his lamp.*
DURATION: *1 minute, 30 seconds*

Overview: Aladdin tells the Genie that he can't set him free. In order to keep up his charade as a prince, he must use all of his wishes on himself, and not use the final one to grant the Genie his freedom.

Illustration: This clip illustrates how quickly lies can grow out of control! More and more lies must be continually piled on top in order to keep the truth hidden—and, as lies become larger, more people are affected and get hurt. Confessing lies as quickly as possible is the best for everyone, including the liar.

Questions
- **Did you ever have a small lie grow bigger? What happened?**
- **What would have happened if you'd told the truth in the beginning? How would the consequences have been different?**

- Why are lies so destructive? Have you ever been hurt by someone else's lie?

    Read Colossians 3:9-10.

- In what ways is lying contrary to the "new self" we find in God?
- What lies do you need to confess?

LYING—Saving Face

Title: A BUG'S LIFE (G)

Scripture: Proverbs 12:22

Alternate Takes: Selfishness (1 Corinthians 10:24), Integrity (Proverbs 20:7)

START TIME: *1 hour, 00 minutes, 15 seconds*
START CUE: *Princess Atta confronts Flik.*
END TIME: *1 hour, 2 minutes, 00 seconds*
END CUE: *Flik apologizes and leaves.*
DURATION: *1 minute, 45 seconds*

Overview: Princess Atta discovers that the "warriors" who are supposed to defend them from the grasshoppers are actually common circus performers. The Queen chastises Flik for lying to them and for putting his personal fear of rejection over the needs and safety of the entire colony. Princess Atta banishes Flik from the colony because of his blatant disregard for the truth and the safety of the others.

Illustration: We're all familiar with lying to save face (because of other people who do it to us, of course). Our lies eventually find us out. When a lie is mainly to save face, we end up looking worse than if we'd spoken the truth in the first place. Even worse, our lies often affect other people negatively and reveal our selfish heart. This illustration can get kids gabbin' about the consequences of saving face.

Questions
- What would have happened if Flik had confessed his mistake in the beginning?
- Have you ever tried to save face by telling a lie? What happened?
- Why is it so tempting to try to save face?

    Read Proverbs 12:22.

- What are the benefits of being completely honest, even when it's hard?
- In what areas of your life do you need to live more truthfully?

LYING—Moooooommm...

Title: FERRIS BUELLER'S DAY OFF (PG-13)

Scripture: Ephesians 6:2-3

Alternate Takes: Abundant Life (Ecclesiastes 5:18),
Knowledge (Ecclesiastes 2:12-13)

START TIME: *3 minutes, 30 seconds*
START CUE: *Ferris explains how he fakes illness.*
END TIME: *4 minutes, 45 seconds*
END CUE: *Ferris goes to take a shower.*
DURATION: *1 minute, 15 seconds*

Overview: Ferris Bueller explains how he fakes being sick when he wants to stay home from school. He claims he must do this in order to enjoy a beautiful day.

Illustration: None of us would *ever* lie to our parents. (Mom, I hope you're not reading this.) Unfortunately people do lie, but it doesn't make it right. God wants us to live truthful lives, especially with our parents (the whole honor thing). This scene shows our playful attitude about lies—an attitude that God doesn't share.

Questions
- **Have you ever faked being sick? Did it work?**
- **Have your parents ever caught you in a lie? How did they act?**
  Read Ephesians 6:2-3.
- **What do honesty and honoring your parents have to do with each other?**
- **How does honesty affect your relationship with your parents?**
- **What things do you need to start being more honest with them about?**

MATERIALISM—Image Is Everything

Title: WAYNE'S WORLD (PG-13)

Scripture: 1 John 2:15-17

Alternate Take: Appearances (1 Samuel 16:7)

START TIME: *48 minutes, 00 seconds*
START CUE: *Benjamin approaches Wayne and Garth.*
END TIME: *49 minutes, 15 seconds*
END CUE: *Benjamin leaves Wayne and Garth alone.*
DURATION: *1 minute, 15 seconds*

Overview: Wayne and Garth do over-the-top product placement endorsements, while telling their producer Benjamin that they'll never sell out their artistic integrity.

Themes L-Q

Illustration: I can see it now: This sermon was brought to you by Pepsi, the choice of God's children. (I have actually seen Scripture toilet paper. Whoever came up with *that* idea has *a lot* of explaining to do.) Advertising surrounds and bombards us with messages every minute. Advertising fuels our materialistic desires. God, however, continues to be old school, preaching contentment in the face of the American Dream. Use this clip to get kids thinking about how they deal with materialistic messages and desires.

Questions
- **What is your favorite commercial?**
- **How does advertising affect you?**
- **Do you think Jesus would advertise if he came to earth today? Why or why not?**
  Read 1 John 2:15-17.
- **What happens to people who fall in love with the world in both their physical and spiritual lives?**
- **How can you guard your heart from the influences of materialism?**

MERCY—You're Letting Me Go?

Title: YOU'VE GOT MAIL (PG)

Scripture: John 8:3-11

Alternate Take: Kindness (Colossians 3:12-14)

START TIME: *42 minutes, 15 seconds*
START CUE: *Kathleen checks out at the grocery store.*
END TIME: *44 minutes, 00 seconds*
END CUE: *Kathleen exits.*
DURATION: *1 minute, 45 seconds*

Overview: Kathleen wants to pay for her groceries with a credit card in the "cash only" line. Rose, the cashier, refuses, until Joe comes over and sweet-talks her into making an exception for Kathleen.

Illustration: This small expression of mercy is just a glimpse of the mercy God has for us. We deserve death for our sin, but Christ's blood always allows the mercy to roll down over us. We extend mercy because we received more mercy than we can ever repay. This simple clip will shine a spotlight on mercy and the role it plays in our faith.

Questions
- **What does the word "mercy" mean?**
- **When was the last time you received mercy from someone? When have you extended mercy?**

Read John 8:3-11.

- **What impact do you think Jesus' words and actions had on this woman's life?**
- **How has God been merciful to you? How have you responded?**
- **Who do you need to extend mercy to and how can you do that?**

MISTAKES—Remember the Time...

Title: RUNAWAY BRIDE (PG)

Scripture: Romans 3:23

Alternate Takes: Forgiveness (Philippians 3:13-14), Judging (Matthew 7:3-5)

START TIME: *1 hour, 10 minutes, 45 seconds*
START CUE: *The wedding party calls for a toast.*
END TIME: *1 hour, 13 minutes, 00 seconds*
END CUE: *The wedding party stops roasting Maggie.*
DURATION: *2 minutes, 15 seconds*

Overview: Maggie gets roasted by her wedding party, and people make jokes about how she always runs away and leaves men standing at the altar. Ike stands up for Maggie when he makes a toast to the wedding party and tells them that he hopes someone rubs *their* noses in *their* mistakes.

Illustration: *Everybody* makes mistakes (a pretty safe generalization). Mistakes themselves aren't so bad because we can learn a lot from them. The problem is that people never forget them! Shaking the memory of a mistake can take a lifetime. At least God forgets our mistakes when we ask him to (if only people would be more like him!).

Questions
- **Have you made a mistake that no one will let you forget?**
- **How does that make you feel?**
- **Why do people like to bring up each other's mistakes?**
    Read Romans 3:23.
- **How does this verse affect your view of mistakes?**
- **How can you move on from past mistakes?**

Q-L

OBEDIENCE—Step to It!

Title: THE MAN WHO KNEW TOO LITTLE (PG)

Scripture: Matthew 4:18-22

Alternate Take: Helping Others (Deuteronomy 22:4)

START TIME: *23 minutes, 30 seconds*
START CUE: *Wally messes around outside.*
END TIME: *24 minutes, 30 seconds*
END CUE: *Wally saves the day.*
DURATION: *1 minute*

Overview: Wally Ritchie lackadaisically responds to a woman's screams for help, oblivious to the true urgency of the situation. He finally arrives and saves her, but he is almost too late.

Illustration: Unfortunately, we sometimes respond to God's call with the same "zeal" that Wally exhibits in this clip. When God directs us to act, we often sit and question the call—afraid or unwilling to move. When God tells us to jump, we should ask "How high?" and not "What's in it for me?" Our delay not only looks foolish to God, but we risk completely missing out on joining God's work. Use this scene to highlight the importance of responding to God immediately.

Questions
- **Have you ever had someone respond slowly to a crisis you were in? What happened?**
- **How have you responded to God's call in the past? Why?**
  Read Matthew 4:18-22.
- **Would you respond as quickly to Jesus as the disciples did? Why or why not?**
- **What can happen when we wait to obey God?**
- **What can you do to drop the "nets" that are holding you back from responding to God in your life?**

OMNISCIENCE—Looking Over Your Shoulder

Title: THE PRINCESS BRIDE (PG)

Scripture: 1 John 3:18-20

Alternate Takes: Integrity (1 Timothy 3:7-10), Pride (Proverbs 29:23)

START TIME: *10 minutes, 00 seconds*
START CUE: *Montoya looks behind the boat.*
END TIME: *11 minutes, 15 seconds*
END CUE: *Princess Buttercup jumps into the water.*
DURATION: *1 minute, 15 seconds*

Overview: Montoya and Vizzini take the kidnapped Princess Buttercup with them across the sea. Montoya keeps looking back to see if anyone is following them, even though Vizzini swears no one could have seen them. But Vizzini discovers, much to his surprise, that someone did see them and is pursuing them.

Illustration: Even though Vizzini thought he'd escaped without being seen, somehow a mysterious man in black was able to follow them. Use this scene to prompt a discussion about how God really sees everything we do—nothing is hidden from him. We can hide things from our friends, but not from God. Since our hidden life will be revealed, we should always live with integrity.

Questions
- **When you were younger, did you ever think you got away with something, but didn't? What happened? How did you get caught?**
- **Have you ever wished God wasn't watching you? Why did you feel that way?**
- **Why do we try to hide things from God?**
  Read 1 John 3:18-20.
- **Does realizing that God knows everything set your heart at rest? Why or why not?**
- **What will you change in your daily life to better honor our God who sees everything?**

PARENTS—But You Promised!

Title: HOPE FLOATS (PG-13)

Scripture: Luke 11:11-13

Alternate Takes: Trust (Isaiah 2:22), Divorce (Malachi 2:13-16)

START TIME: *1 hour, 42 minutes, 15 seconds*
START CUE: *Bernice follows her father to his car.*
END TIME: *1 hour, 44 minutes, 15 seconds*
END CUE: *Bernice's dad drives away, leaving her crying.*
DURATION: *2 minutes*

Overview: Bernice attempts to go home with her father, clinging to his promise that she can live with him whenever she wants. Her confusion turns to heartbreak as he drives away and promises her that he loves her, even though he does not want her in his life at the moment.

Illustration: It's impossible to see this clip and not get choked up. Neglectful or abusive parents can warp their children's view of God. A distrust of our heavenly Father often follows from the failures and broken promises of earthly fathers. Though this is a tough subject for some people, prayer and love can restore a proper image and trust of God.

Questions
- **How did this clip make you feel?**
- **Has a family member ever made you feel this way? What happened?**
- **Have you been able to forgive them? Why or why not?**
    Read Luke 11:11-13.
- **Do you believe God's intentions for you are good?**
- **How can you find healing from God in hurtful situations?**

PARENTS—Dealing With Dad

Title: BIG DADDY (PG-13)

Scripture: 1 Corinthians 8:6
Alternate Takes: Encouragement (Ephesians 4:29), Father's Influence (1 Kings 15:26)

START TIME: *36 minutes, 30 seconds*
START CUE: *Sonny and his son sit down.*
END TIME: *37 minutes, 15 seconds*
END CUE: *The "freak" walks away.*
DURATION: *45 seconds*

Overview: Sonny tells his adopted son that fathers just screw up their kids and claims that every screwed up guy blames his father for his condition. Sonny points out a "freak" walking by and tells the guy to get over his father, causing him to burst into tears.

Illustration: Leave it to Adam Sandler to make us laugh at such a depressing topic. Many wounded people have issues now because of a broken relationship with their earthly father, which in turn affects their relationship with the heavenly Father.

Questions
- **What impact has your father had on your life?**
- **How does your father affect your view of God?**
    Read 1 Corinthians 8:6.
- **Do you like to think of God as your father? Why or why not?**
- **How can people without fathers find healing?**
- **How can you change your attitude about your father? How can you help others change their attitudes about their fathers?**

PARENTS—Shhhh!

Title: AUSTIN POWERS: INTERNATIONAL MAN OF MYSTERY (PG-13)

Scripture: Ephesians 6:1-4

Alternate Takes: Listening (Proverbs 19:20), Obedience (Exodus 20:12)

START TIME: *1 hour, 5 minutes, 45 seconds*
START CUE: *Dr. Evil says, "You just don't get it."*
END TIME: *1 hour, 6 minutes, 15 seconds*
END CUE: *Scott remains silent.*
DURATION: *30 seconds*

Overview: Dr. Evil does not want any advice from his son Scott. Every time Scott attempts to utter a word, Dr. Evil cuts him off with a "Shhh" and a cutting hand motion. Scott, completely frustrated, finally gives up on trying to communicate with his father.

Illustration: It may be hard to believe, but parents can sometimes be wrong. God commands us to honor our parents, even when we feel frustrated or infuriated. Though parents may sometimes pass down edicts without discussion, teens must refocus their attitudes and communicate with their parents through the right actions of honor and obedience. Simple rebellion may seem more fun, but we've got to honor our parents even if they completely frustrate us.

Questions
- **Can you relate to this scene? How?**
- **What are some other ways your parents frustrate you?**
- **How do you react to them when you feel frustrated?**
  Read Ephesians 6:1-4.
- **How can you talk to your parents about your frustration?**
- **What are some ways to change your negative attitudes toward your parents?**

PARENTS—Stop Embarrassing Me!

Title: SOME KIND OF WONDERFUL (PG-13)

Scripture: Proverbs 30:17

Alternate Take: Pleasing Others (Mark 15:15)

START TIME: *12 minutes, 00 seconds*
START CUE: *Mr. Nelson waves to Laura in her class.*
END TIME: *12 minutes, 45 seconds*
END CUE: *Laura asks if she can see the nurse.*
DURATION: *45 seconds*

Overview: Mr. Nelson waves to his daughter Laura in her classroom. She screams like she's in a horror movie when she sees him and he leaves the window. Laura tries to act as if nothing happened and asks to see the nurse.

Illustration: Parents can be soooooo embarrassing! (My dad still wears Sansabelt pants.) Our parents sacrifice, sweat, and cry over us, and we often repay them with a cold shoulder in public. Use this clip to get kids thinking about the fact that God gave us a family to enjoy, not to be cool.

Questions
- **What is the most embarrassing thing your parents have ever done?**
- **If you could change something about your parents, what would it be?**
- **What are important qualities for parents to have?**
  Read Proverbs 30:17.
- **What are some subtle ways that you mock your parents? Why is this verse so harsh toward those who mock their parents?**
- **How can you honor your parents this week?**

PEER PRESSURE—I'll Be Your Best Friend

Title: DUMB AND DUMBER (PG-13)

Scripture: Deuteronomy 13:6-8

Alternate Take: Gambling (Luke 16:1-2)

START TIME: *37 minutes, 30 seconds*
START CUE: *Harry wants to bet Lloyd.*
END TIME: *38 minutes, 15 seconds*
END CUE: *Harry says he's gonna trick Lloyd.*
DURATION: *45 seconds*

Overview: Harry wants to bet Lloyd, but Lloyd refuses since he doesn't gamble. Harry tries to pressure Lloyd. Finally, they bet on whether Harry can make Lloyd gamble before the day is through.

Illustration: The film's title gives away something about this scene! Yet, even Harry and Lloyd can teach us a lesson about the persuasive power of peer pressure. Peer pressure takes multiple forms and has various levels of influence, from friends and family members to TV programs and commercials telling us what to do and buy. Thankfully, God's Spirit helps us discern and stand strong in the face of every temptation.

Questions
- **Have you ever pressured someone into doing something? Why?**
- **What types of things do people try to pressure you into doing?**

- How do you deal with peer pressure?
  Read Deuteronomy 13:6-8.
- What should you do when someone tries to entice you to do something wrong?
- How can God help you cope with pressures in the future?

PERSEVERANCE—The Roller Coaster

Title: PARENTHOOD (PG-13)

Scripture: Romans 5:1-5

Alternate Take: Trials (James 1:2-4)

START TIME: *1 hour, 49 minutes, 30 seconds*
START CUE: *Gil says, "I'm still high from the baseball game."*
END TIME: *1 hour, 52 minutes, 15 seconds*
END CUE: *Gil says that his grandmother is sitting in the neighbor's car.*
DURATION: *2 minutes, 45 seconds*

Overview: Gil and Karen disagree about how to view trials. Gil wants to control everything because he doesn't like messes. He fears his children are going to mess up. Karen prefers optimism and says that maybe they won't mess up—and if they do, so what? Gil's grandmother wanders in and says that she always loved roller coasters—the ups and downs—and hated boring merry-go-rounds that just went in circles.

Illustration: There are no guarantees in life. Ups and downs will fill the journey. The times of joy, as well as the trials, make life the wonderful, exciting thing that it is. By trusting God to keep your car on the track, you can concentrate on enjoying the ride, even the valleys. Besides, people who never experience the two ends of the spectrum—both the ups and the downs—never really appreciate living and God's providence.

Questions
- Are you an optimist or a pessimist? Why?
- How has your life been a roller coaster? What has been your highest point so far? your lowest point?
  Read Romans 5:1-5.
- How can you possibly rejoice through the valleys on the roller coaster of life?
- How does God help during times of difficulty?
- What will help you persevere through future times of trouble in life?

POSSESSIONS—Can't Live Without It!

Title: PEE-WEE'S BIG ADVENTURE (PG)

Scripture: Luke 12:16-21

Alternate Take: Idols (Psalm 106:36)

START TIME: *18 minutes, 30 seconds*
START CUE: *Pee-Wee wakes up with police around him.*
END TIME: *21 minutes, 00 seconds*
END CUE: *Pee-Wee stands in front of a bike shop.*
DURATION: *2 minutes, 30 seconds*

Overview: Pee-Wee Herman wanders the streets, hoping for a glimpse of his lost love—his stolen bike. Instead, he only sees constant reminders of it and not the real thing.

Illustration: Pee-Wee may be a little mental here, but many people don't realize how tightly they hold on to their possessions until they break them or lose them. This clip can prompt us to examine our hearts concerning our possessions before we become too attached to those things.

Questions
- Is Pee-Wee's devotion to his bike healthy? Why or why not?
- Do you own anything you love that much?
  Read Luke 12:16-21.
- How are you like the man in this parable?
- When do possessions possess you?
- How can you loosen your grip on your possessions?

PRAYER—Are You Desperate?

Title: MR. HOLLAND'S OPUS (PG)

Scripture: Psalm 42:1-2

Alternate Take: Holy Spirit (Romans 8:26-27)

START TIME: *1 hour, 4 minutes, 00 seconds*
START CUE: *Iris wants to put Cole in a private school.*
END TIME: *1 hour, 5 minutes, 30 seconds*
END CUE: *Iris cries and holds Cole.*
DURATION: *1 minute, 30 seconds*

Overview: Iris tells her husband that they need to put their son Cole (who is deaf) in a private school, but Mr. Holland is concerned about paying for it. Cole motions and yells for something, but Iris can't understand him. Cole throws a fit and Mr. Holland asks what Cole wants. Iris doesn't know, and she yells at her husband and screams, "I want to talk to my son!"

Illustration: If only we had the same burning passion to talk to God! We have the unbelievable opportunity to build a relationship with the God of all creation, yet we take it for granted! Instead of seeing what an awesome privilege it is, many people feel like prayer is a duty. This powerful scene will prompt a conversation about our attitudes toward prayer.

Questions
- Have you ever been unable to communicate with someone? What happened?
- Do you have the same passion to talk to God that Iris had to talk to her son? Why or why not?
  Read Psalm 42:1-2.
- How important was talking to God to the psalmist?
- What are the most important aspects of prayer? What does God care about in our prayers?
- What can you do to make your prayer life more rich and personal?

PRAYER—Fine, Let's Talk

Title: INDIANA JONES AND THE LAST CRUSADE (PG-13)

Scripture: Jeremiah 33:3

Alternate Takes: Parents (Deuteronomy 6:6-7), Anger (Ephesians 4:25-27)

START TIME: *1 hour, 14 minutes, 00 seconds*
START CUE: *Indy sits down with his dad.*
END TIME: *1 hour, 15 minutes, 15 seconds*
END CUE: *Indy doesn't know what to say to his dad.*
DURATION: *1 minute, 15 seconds*

Overview: Indy says he and his dad never talk. They blame each other for their distant relationship, and his dad finally says, "Fine, let's talk." Indy can't think of anything to say, and the argument ends.

Illustration: I love it when people use the excuse "You never call." (My phone has the option to *make* and *receive* calls.) Communication is a two-way street! It works this way not only with our earthly relationships, but with our heavenly one, too. God wants a relationship with a flow of information back and forth. Use this clip to help your kids unveil the challenges and rewards of true communication with God.

Questions

- Have you ever been in a situation like Indy's? Why do we sometimes not communicate with the people we love?
- How do you overcome these communication breakdowns?
- What breaks down your communication with God?
    Read Jeremiah 33:3.
- What is God's role in prayer? Why do you think he wants this type of relationship with us?
- How can you improve your communication with God?

PRAYER—Let's Make a Deal

Title: AMADEUS (PG)

Scripture: Psalm 66:17-19

Alternate Takes: Hate (Matthew 5:21-22), Honoring Parents (Exodus 21:17)

START TIME: *9 minutes, 45 seconds*
START CUE: *Salieri remembers playing as a child.*
END TIME: *12 minutes, 30 seconds*
END CUE: *Salieri thanks God for killing his father.*
DURATION: *2 minutes, 45 seconds*

Overview: Salieri remembers his childhood desire to be a great musician. His father wouldn't let him pursue his dream, so Salieri promised God he would glorify him with his music if he could become a famous composer. God "answered" his prayer by killing Salieri's father.

Illustration: Let's be honest—we've all bartered with God at some point in our lives. (Because we have *soooo* many things that God desperately needs.) Prayer is not a synonym for "Let's Make a Deal." Prayer is how we open ourselves to God's communication and direction, and it's a time to give God the praise he richly deserves. Let's leave the wish list for Santa Claus.

Questions

- Have you ever tried to make a deal with God? What happened?
- How does society view prayer? According to TV and movies, what purpose does prayer serve?
    Read Psalm 66:17-19.
- What kinds of prayers does God *not* listen to?
- Is it OK to ask God for things? Why or why not?
- What changes in your attitude will erase any wickedness in your prayers?

PRAYER—Pray Where You Are

Title: THE OUT-OF-TOWNERS (G)

Scripture: 1 Thessalonians 5:16-18

Alternate Take: Obedience (Mark 12:17)

START TIME: *1 hour, 19 minutes, 15 seconds*
START CUE: *George and Gwen enter the church.*
END TIME: *1 hour, 21 minutes, 15 seconds*
END CUE: *George and Gwen leave the church.*
DURATION: *2 minutes*

Overview: George and Gwen Kellerman enter a church to pray for help and for direction from their disastrous trip to New York. A short, sarcastic argument ensues once they're inside when they learn the church is closed and they cannot pray there.

Illustration: This clip centers on prayer and some of our incorrect beliefs about it. George insists on praying in the church. He loses the argument, is forced outside, and is thus unable to pray. Many people, including students, take this attitude toward their own church building. Many only think about and relate to Jesus while they're inside the church. It's almost as if the building traps Christ inside and that they need to think about Christ only when they're in church with him. Obviously this idea is false, and this clip should highlight its absurdity.

Questions
- **Why didn't George think he could pray anywhere else?**
- **Has anyone ever stopped you from praying? What happened?**
  Read 1 Thessalonians 5:16-18.
- **When and where should you pray?**
- **What does "pray continually" mean practically, and how can you live out this command?**
- **What are some specific times and places you could begin to pray?**

PRAYER—Stop, Drop, and Pray

Title: HOOSIERS (PG)

Scripture: 1 Thessalonians 5:16-18

Alternate Take: God's Glory (Colossians 3:23-24)

START TIME: *27 minutes, 00 seconds*
START CUE: *The basketball team bows to pray.*
END TIME: *27 minutes, 45 seconds*
END CUE: *The team leaves Strap alone in the locker room, still praying.*
DURATION: *45 seconds*

Overview: The basketball team prays briefly before their first game. The minister says "amen" and everyone gets up and heads for the floor except Strap, who continues to pray by himself.

Illustration: Prayer is like the ultimate cellular phone. You have it with you at all times and you can use it whenever you want. The best part is that God always answers your call, day or night. We should exercise the privilege of prayer more often and seek God continuously.

Questions
- **Where is the strangest place you have ever prayed?**
- **What made you decide to pray then, and how did God answer?**
- **What amazes you most about prayer?**
     Read 1 Thessalonians 5:16-18.
- **When and where can you pray this week that you normally don't?**
- **How can you get more out of your prayer time this week?**

PRAYER—Who Ya Gonna Call?

Title: THE SURE THING (PG-13)

Scripture: Psalm 18:2-6

Alternate Takes: Thankfulness (1 Thessalonians 5:18), Grumbling (Philippians 2:14)

START TIME: *57 minutes, 30 seconds*
START CUE: *Gib asks Alison for some gum.*
END TIME: *1 hour, 00 minutes, 00 seconds*
END CUE: *Alison realizes she has a credit card.*
DURATION: *2 minutes, 30 seconds*

Overview: Gib and Alison sit in the middle of nowhere with no food, money, or transportation. Gib whines until Alison snaps, "Things can be worse!" A flash flood and no shelter make it worse, until Alison suddenly remembers that she has a credit card.

Illustration: This scene is over the top, but it mirrors how we often respond to trials. Hardship hits, we complain. Things grow worse, we desperately seek solutions. Once we hit rock bottom, we think, "Hey, maybe I should ask God!" and we realize he has been there the whole time.

Questions
- **What is the worst situation of bad luck you have ever been in? What happened?**

- **Did you immediately turn to God for help or did you wait? Why?**
  Read Psalm 18:2-6.
- **Why do we forget to include God as our refuge and shield in our lives?**
- **What does it take for you to get God involved in your life?**
- **How will turning to him *first* make your life easier?**

PRESSURE—You Can Do Better

Title: PARENTHOOD (PG-13)

Scripture: 2 Corinthians 13:11

Alternate Take: Excellence (1 Thessalonians 4:1-2)

START TIME: *12 minutes, 45 seconds*
START CUE: *Helen calls her sister.*
END TIME: *14 minutes, 00 seconds*
END CUE: *Patty agrees to try harder.*
DURATION: *1 minute, 15 seconds*

Overview: Helen calls her sister Susan to see how Susan's daughter Patty is doing academically. Susan says Patty has been slacking and that her husband Nathan is having a talk with her. Nathan tells Patty she'll have to pick up the pace if she wants to get into a good college, so he'd appreciate her trying harder. Patty, who is four years old, agrees.

Illustration: It's hard to believe, but some kids get tons of pressure from their parents to succeed. (No dinner until you shoot one hundred more free throws!) This scene takes parental pressure to a hilarious extreme, but it will spark a discussion on a heavy topic.

Questions
- **What things do your parents or others pressure you about?**
- **Do you put pressure on yourself? Why?**
  Read 2 Corinthians 13:11.
- **What does "aim for perfection" mean? Will we hit it?**
- **How can we have the peace of God while aiming for perfection?**
- **How can you talk to the people who put pressure on you and begin to live with the peace of God?**

PRIDE—I Will Never Do Fast Food

Title: REALITY BITES (PG-13)

Scripture: Jeremiah 49:16

Alternate Takes: Work (2 Thessalonians 3:10-12), Service (Colossians 3:23)

START TIME: *46 minutes, 30 seconds*
START CUE: *Lelaina asks her father for a loan.*
END TIME: *48 minutes, 45 seconds*
END CUE: *Lelaina's fast food interview ends.*
DURATION: *2 minutes, 15 seconds*

Overview: Lelaina's father refuses to give her a loan and tells her to get a job. She complains that, as a valedictorian, she deserves a "good" job. He says she has to lower herself. She does and fails miserably in her interview at a fast food restaurant.

Illustration: We all deserve to be the CEO since of course we're more intelligent and experienced than anyone above us. So many tasks, such as chores and homework, seem "beneath us," but Christians are called to serve. By deflating our pride, we can perform any job, whether we're paid or not, with a light heart.

Questions
- **What is the worst job or task you've ever had? Why was it so bad?**
- **What could you have done to make it better?**
  Read Jeremiah 49:16.
- **Why should we view ourselves in humility?**
- **How can you turn unenjoyable tasks into meaningful, fulfilling work?**
- **What distasteful job do you have now that you need to improve your attitude toward?**

PRIDE—Puffed Daddy

Title: THE WIZARD OF OZ (G)

Scripture: Proverbs 11:2

Alternate Take: Appearances (1 Samuel 16:7)

START TIME: *1 hour, 28 minutes, 15 seconds*
START CUE: *Toto exposes Oz.*
END TIME: *1 hour, 29 minutes, 15 seconds*
END CUE: *Oz admits that he's a sham.*
DURATION: *1 minute*

Overview: Oz is talking about how great and amazing he is when Toto pulls back the curtain to reveal…a man. Oz is a mere human with nothing but illusions up his sleeve and hot air in his breath.

Illustration: We've all known people who go *on* and *on* about their talents until they have to put up the goods. Empty boasts are always found out in the long run. People who are for real don't need to talk—they prove themselves through their actions.

Questions
- **How do you feel about braggarts?**
- **Do people ever think you boast about yourself? Why?**
- **What has happened to the prideful people you know?**
  Read Proverbs 11:2.
- **What are some of the challenges of being humble? What are some of the benefits?**
- **How can you be more humble in your life?**

PRIDE—The Harder They Fall

Title: THE PRINCESS BRIDE (PG)

Scripture: Proverbs 16:18

Alternate Take: Knowledge (1 Corinthians 8:1b-2)

START TIME: *31 minutes, 30 seconds*
START CUE: *Westley sets the goblets on the table.*
END TIME: *34 minutes, 15 seconds*
END CUE: *Vizzini keels over dead.*
DURATION: *2 minutes, 45 seconds*

Overview: Vizzini and Westley face off in a battle of the wits for possession of Princess Buttercup by choosing a glass to drink, one of which is poisoned. Before deciding, Vizzini crows about his superior intellect.

Illustration: It's so stupid to brag about our talents and abilities because God is the one who gives these gifts in the first place! This ridiculous scene shows how pride in one's abilities can cause the ultimate fall.

Questions
- **When does confidence become pride?**
- **Do you take pride in your greatest talent? Why? Where do your talents come from?**
- **Has your talent ever failed you? How?**
  Read Proverbs 16:18.

- **What happens to prideful people? Can you think of one real-life example of this verse?**
- **How can you remain humble?**

PRIDE—Pushing to the Front

Title: MUPPET TREASURE ISLAND (G)

Scripture: Luke 14:8-11

Alternate Take: Mercy (1 Samuel 24:1-17)

START TIME: *1 hour, 26 minutes, 00 seconds*
START CUE: *Kermit hops over to Long John Silver.*
END TIME: *1 hour, 27 minutes, 15 seconds*
END CUE: *Kermit loses his sword.*
DURATION: *1 minute, 15 seconds*

Overview: Kermit hops over to Long John Silver for a sword fight. Kermit proves to be extremely skillful in swordplay. After bragging about his skills, however, he immediately loses his sword.

Illustration: Ouch! Unfortunately this is a common scenario. Just when you get confidence in yourself, God lets you fall on your face to remind you who's really calling the shots. Let's try to learn the lesson from Kermit this time so we don't have to go through a similar situation.

Questions
- **Have you ever fallen flat in an activity you were confident you could do? What happened?**
- **Why did you fail at something you are gifted in?**
  Read Luke 14:8-11.
- **Why do we exalt ourselves with the talents God gave us in the first place?**
- **How can you move from pride to humility?**
- **What is one way you can use your talents to glorify God instead of yourself?**

PURPOSE—This Empty Life

Title: REALITY BITES (PG-13)

Scripture: Jeremiah 29:11

Alternate Take: Tragedy (Romans 8:28)

START TIME: *32 minutes, 15 seconds*
START CUE: *Troy tells about his father's cancer.*

END TIME: *33 minutes, 30 seconds*
END CUE: *Troy finishes his video interview.*
DURATION: *1 minute, 15 seconds*

Overview: Troy spouts his view of life in a video interview. He believes that life is empty, meaningless, and dispenses random bits of tragedy. Therefore, happiness can only be gained in brief, simple moments.

Illustration: I think this character would say the glass is half empty. Many people have a bleak outlook on life. After all, without Jesus, I honestly don't see much reason for optimism. That is why we must share the joy of the Lord and share that life has richness and depth in Christ. This clip will get kids thinking about the purpose they have in life and the need for them to share that purpose with others.

Questions

- Do you enjoy being around people who are pessimistic? Why or why not?
- How do you relate to people with that kind of view of the world?
  Read Jeremiah 29:11.
- How does God give meaning to life?
- As a Christian, how would you explain tragedies?
- How can you show God's joy to people?

Movie Illustration
THEMES R-Z

Racism...Substance Abuse...Witnessing

RACISM—People Are People

Title: THE MISSION (PG)

Scripture: Colossians 3:9-11

Alternate Take: Pride (Philippians 2:3)

START TIME: *54 minutes, 15 seconds*
START CUE: *A native boy sings.*
END TIME: *55 minutes, 45 seconds*
END CUE: *The aristocrat finishes speaking.*
DURATION: *1 minute, 30 seconds*

Overview: A native child sings a beautiful song for the cardinal and the aristocrats. The cardinal comments on the boy's amazing skill, and an aristocrat responds that the child has merely learned tricks like an animal and is not worth as much as educated and cultured men.

Illustration: I want to jump inside this movie and give this guy a piece of my mind! (Oh yeah…it's only acting.) Unfortunately, many people today have similar racist attitudes, although they don't necessarily express them. Racism stems from the belief that some people are worth more than others because of their race; people can be prejudiced against others for a variety of reasons, though, including culture, economic status, and education. Yet God sees no divisions between people—all are sinners and in need of his grace. This disturbing clip will prompt a serious discussion on this prevalent problem.

Questions
- **Why did the man believe that the child was just an animal? How did this clip make you feel?**
- **How and where is racism alive today? What are some examples you've observed?**
- **Where does racism come from?**
   Read Colossians 3:9-11.
- **What should be our response to racism or prejudice?**
- **What are some ways you can fight racism in your everyday life?**

RATIONALIZING SIN—We're Doing the Right Thing

Title: RAISING ARIZONA (PG-13)

Scripture: Isaiah 5:20

Alternate Take: Covetousness (Exodus 20:17)

START TIME: *17 minutes, 45 seconds*
START CUE: *Hi enters the car with the baby.*
END TIME: *18 minutes, 30 seconds*
END CUE: *Hi and Ed plan for their new family.*
DURATION: *45 seconds*

Overview: Hi gets into the car with the baby he just kidnapped. Ed holds the boy and bursts into tears because she "loves him so much!" She has a second of remorse, but then she quickly explains away the crime and convinces herself that she and Hi are actually good Samaritans.

Illustration: Obviously, kidnapping is a horrible thing to do. Hi and Ed convince themselves otherwise, which is why this clip is a great example of rationalization. This example highlights a cultural trend: People rarely engage in sin without first convincing themselves that their actions are OK in a particular situation. This clip will help teenagers evaluate their own tendency to explain away their sinful thoughts and actions.

Questions
- **When have you rationalized a sin? What reasons did you give?**
- **What happened?**
    Read Isaiah 5:20.
- **Do you know anyone who does this? What do other people think of them?**
- **How does rationalizing sins, even small ones, affect your life?**
- **What will you do to stop rationalizing sin?**

REDEMPTION—It Ain't Over 'til the Angels Sing

Title: RETURN OF THE JEDI (PG)

Scripture: Luke 23:39-43

Alternate Take: Sin Nature (Ephesians 4:18)

START TIME: *1 hour, 22 minutes, 45 seconds*
START CUE: *Luke and Darth Vader talk alone.*
END TIME: *1 hour, 25 minutes, 00 seconds*
END CUE: *Darth Vader turns his back on Luke.*
DURATION: *2 minutes, 15 seconds*

Overview: Luke talks with Darth Vader, his father, challenging him to turn from his evil ways. Luke believes his father still has good in him—it's only buried under years of wickedness. Vader flatly states that it is too late for him to find redemption.

Themes R-Z

Illustration: So many people appear to be beyond God's ability to save. Satan convinces people that, through their years of sin, they have built walls that are too thick for God to break down to offer forgiveness. And some Christians believe that a few sinners are so evil that God could never draw them close. The truth is that *all* people can be saved, no matter what their past deeds are—they must only repent in the present and turn to Jesus for forgiveness.

Questions
- **Are there people who are so evil that they cannot be saved? Who?**
- **Is it ever too late for anyone to accept God's forgiveness? Why or why not?**
  Read Luke 23:39-43.
- **Why does God forgive even people who have rebelled against him their entire lives?**
- **How could you share God's love with someone who is ashamed of his or her sin?**
- **Who can you share this good news with this week?**

REJECTION—She Loves Me Not

Title: THE WEDDING SINGER (PG-13)

Scripture: Genesis 29:22-30

Alternate Take: Tragedy (1 Chronicles 16:11)

START TIME: *15 minutes, 30 seconds*
START CUE: *Robbie stands with the minister for his wedding.*
END TIME: *17 minutes, 30 seconds*
END CUE: *Robbie smashes a mirror in frustration.*
DURATION: *2 minutes*

Overview: Robbie waits for his fiancée, Linda, to show up for their wedding. His sister tells him that Linda isn't coming to the wedding. Robbie says he'll be OK—he just needs to be alone. Then he throws a mirror in the waiting room in anger at the rejection he feels.

Illustration: Imagine if you threw a party and everyone came except your bride! Robbie experiences one of the most profound forms of rejection possible when he's left at the altar. We all know that rejection in any form is not easy. That's why we must rely on God's perfect love to ease the blow of rejection.

Questions
- **Have you ever been rejected? What happened? How did you deal with it?**

- **What people in your life will never reject you?**
- **Why will they never reject you?**
  Read Genesis 29:22-30.
- **How can God heal feelings of rejection like those Leah must have felt?**
- **How does God's love give you confidence in the face of rejection?**

REVENGE—Gotta Have It

Title: BATMAN FOREVER (PG-13)

Scripture: Deuteronomy 32:35

Alternate Take: Anger (Ephesians 4:31-32)

START TIME: *1 hour, 8 minutes, 30 seconds*
START CUE: *Robin confronts Batman in the bat cave.*
END TIME: *1 hour, 10 minutes, 15 seconds*
END CUE: *Robin storms out.*
DURATION: *1 minute, 45 seconds*

Overview: Robin asks Batman for help in finding Two-Face and killing him to avenge his family's murder. Batman refuses to help because he knows revenge never ends—it only grows and expands.

Illustration: Here Batman explains the dangers of revenge—how it grows and finally consumes the person who seeks it. God reserves vengeance for himself for this very reason. Only forgiveness can heal a vengeful heart.

Questions
- **Is Robin justified in wanting to kill Two-Face? Why or why not?**
- **Have you ever wanted revenge? What happened?**
- **What does revenge accomplish?**
  Read Deuteronomy 32:35.
- **Why should we leave revenge to the Lord?**
- **Who do you need to forgive in order to destroy the seeds of vengeance in your life?**

SACRIFICE—He Took My Place

Title: BEAUTY AND THE BEAST (G)

Scripture: 1 Peter 1:17-19

Alternate Take: Love (John 15:13)

START TIME: *22 minutes, 30 seconds*
START CUE: *Belle begs the Beast to free her father.*
END TIME: *23 minutes, 45 seconds*
END CUE: *The Beast throws Belle in the cell.*
DURATION: *1 minute, 15 seconds*

Overview: Belle begs the Beast to release her father. The Beast refuses until Belle offers to take her father's place as a prisoner. The Beast agrees, releasing her father and locking up Belle.

Illustration: Though this scene can't compare to the immensity of Christ's sacrifice for us on the cross, the scene does provide a symbolic glimpse at what Jesus did. We were prisoners in sin; Jesus took our place as a prisoner so that we could be free. By taking our place, Jesus Christ exhibited the greatest love in history.

Questions
- **Would you have done what Belle did to save someone you love? Why or why not?**
- **Would you have done it to save someone you didn't like or someone who was mean to you? Why or why not?**
- **Has anyone ever sacrificed something for your sake? What happened and how did that sacrifice make you feel?**
  Read 1 Peter 1:17-19.
- **How does it make you feel when you remember that Jesus died in your place? Can we ever repay Jesus?**
- **What can you do now to show Jesus that you love him and that you're grateful for his sacrifice?**

SACRIFICE—Just Like Jesus

Title: STAR TREK II: THE WRATH OF KHAN (PG)

Scripture: Romans 5:14-19

Alternate Take: Friendship (John 15:13)

START TIME: *1 hour, 36 minutes, 15 seconds*
START CUE: *McCoy and Scotty stop Captain Kirk.*
END TIME: *1 hour, 39 minutes, 15 seconds*
END CUE: *Kirk slumps down next to Mr. Spock.*
DURATION: *3 minutes*

Overview: Spock sacrifices his life so that the entire crew of the Enterprise will live. He tells Kirk that the needs of the many outweigh the needs of the few—or the one.

Illustration: You can love Mr. Spock or hate him, but you can't deny the Christlike sacrifice he makes for the crew of the Enterprise. (I know, I know, he's just a character—he's not real.) Spock's example is a great bridge to a discussion of how Jesus forfeited his life and his glory as God's Son so that many (all of humanity) might be saved.

Questions

- When has someone sacrificed something for you? What happened?
- How have you sacrificed for other people?
- How was Mr. Spock's sacrifice similar to what Jesus did on the cross?
  Read Romans 5:14-19.
- What did Jesus sacrifice so that we might be saved? How does this make you feel?
- How can you show Jesus your thankfulness this week?

SALVATION—The Chosen One

Title: THE FRESHMAN (PG)

Scripture: 2 Thessalonians 2:13

Alternate Take: Assurance (Romans 8:38-39)

START TIME: *1 hour, 1 minute, 15 seconds*
START CUE: *Clark and Tina walk toward his car.*
END TIME: *1 hour, 2 minutes, 15 seconds*
END CUE: *Tina moves to get into the car.*
DURATION: *1 minute*

Overview: Tina tells Clark that he was not robbed randomly. Her father chose Clark before he even moved to New York, handpicking him to become part of their mob "family."

Illustration: *Fuhgeddaboudit!* Though I certainly don't consider being part of God's family like being in the mafia (though if God talked like Brando, that would be cool!), the sentiment in this scene reflects biblical truth. God chose each of us to be part of his family—a spiritual, eternal family. Talk about becoming the ultimate "made man"!

Questions

- Have any of you been handpicked for something? What was it?
- How did being chosen make you feel?
- Were any of you adopted? What is that like?
  Read 2 Thessalonians 2:13.
- What does this verse tell you about salvation?
- How will knowing you are chosen by God affect your daily life?

SEEKING GOD—God-Shaped Hole

Title: REALITY BITES (PG-13)

Scripture: Ecclesiastes 3:10-11

Alternate Take: Afterlife (Revelation 14:13)

START TIME: *1 hour, 23 minutes, 45 seconds*
START CUE: *Troy exits the club onto the street.*
END TIME: *1 hour, 25 minutes, 00 seconds*
END CUE: *Troy walks away.*
DURATION: *1 minute, 15 seconds*

Overview: Troy joins Michael on the street looking for Lelaina. Troy says he doesn't care about finding Lelaina since everyone dies alone. Michael says, "If you really believe that, who are you lookin' for?"

Illustration: "I don't believe in God." People say that all the time! Yet their actions drown our their words when these "atheists" cry out to God for help or blame him in times of tragedy. This scene will get kids thinking about how humans are spiritual beings who instinctively seek to worship God—whether they admit it or not.

Questions
- **What things do people look for in life?**
- **What reasons do people give for not believing in God?**
    Read Ecclesiastes 3:10-11.
- **What do you think it means when it says that God has "set eternity in the hearts of men"?**
- **How do you see the truth of this verse reflected in your friends' lives or the lives of people at school?**
- **How can you share your faith with people who don't believe in God?**

SELF-ESTEEM—My Identity?

Title: CAN'T HARDLY WAIT (PG-13)

Scripture: Colossians 2:9-10

Alternate Take: Fear (Psalm 37:28)

START TIME: *36 minutes, 45 seconds*
START CUE: *Amanda tells her cousin about her breakup.*
END TIME: *38 minutes, 15 seconds*
END CUE: *Amanda says she wants to discover her identity.*
DURATION: *1 minute, 30 seconds*

Overview: Amanda tells her cousin about her breakup with Mike, her boyfriend of four years. She can't really remember why she went out with him for so long. She enjoyed the popularity, but she realized that her whole identity was wrapped up in him. She stayed with him because she feared becoming a nobody again.

Illustration: It's disturbing that this scene really rings true. So many people become consumed with their dating relationships that they cease to exist as individuals. They become a new organism—"us." While relationships are fine, they should never supersede our relationship with our heavenly Father. He created each of us uniquely to serve him, not to become consumed by another person.

Questions
- **Do you know people who have lost their identity in dating relationships? What happened?**
- **When does a relationship move from healthy to unhealthy?**
  Read Colossians 2:9-10.
- **What does having "fullness in Christ" mean?**
- **How should having fullness in Christ affect your friendships and dating relationships?**
- **How can you keep your different relationships balanced?**

SIN—Heavier Than Big Momma

Title: THE MISSION (PG)

Scripture: 2 Timothy 2:25-26

Alternate Takes: Forgiveness (Isaiah 44:21-22), Salvation (Colossians 1:13-14)

START TIME: *32 minutes, 45 seconds*
START CUE: *Mendoza drags his burden.*
END TIME: *34 minutes, 45 seconds*
END CUE: *Mendoza retrieves his burden.*
DURATION: *2 minutes*

Themes R-Z

Overview: Mendoza physically drags his armor and weapons behind him through the wilderness as penance for his life of wickedness. He feels tremendous guilt because he murdered his own brother. When he can't move any farther, the priests cut him free from his burden. Mendoza, though, returns to his burden, picks it up, and continues to carry it.

Illustration: Let's hear it for grace! This clip portrays a vivid image of sin. Many people lug their crimes along with them throughout their life, barely able to drag the weight. Even when they learn that freedom from the weight is possible, they return to their guilt and continue to shoulder the burden, refusing to let it go. Use this scene to illustrate the freedom of living in grace.

Questions
- **What is the heaviest thing you've ever had to carry?**
- **Why do you think Mendoza wanted to keep carrying the burden? How is the bundle of armor like sin?**
  Read 2 Timothy 2:25-26.
- **How can someone escape the "trap of the devil"?**
- **Why do people refuse to let go of their past sins even though they've been forgiven?**
- **How do you need to leave past mistakes behind and move forward in freedom? What is one step you will take this week?**

SIN—On a Scale of 1-10...

Title: RUNAWAY BRIDE (PG)

Scripture: 1 John 3:4

Alternate Takes: Hate (1 John 3:15),
Prayer (Psalm 66:18-19)

START TIME: *31 minutes, 15 seconds*
START CUE: *Maggie enters the confessional.*
END TIME: *32 minutes, 00 seconds*
END CUE: *Priest Brian closes the partition door.*
DURATION: *45 seconds*

Overview: Maggie enters the confessional to ask Priest Brian about the severity of her sin. She wants to destroy the reporter Ike and wonders how bad of a sin that is.

Illustration: God doesn't rate sins like you would rate a talent show. "Hmmm, it didn't hurt anyone directly, and he's sorry for his sin, so it's only a 2." Sin is sin, and it's hard for a performance-driven society to accept that God hates all sins equally (surely he hates murder more than something petty like gossip, right?). Use this clip to emphasize that *all* sins are equally wrong in God's eyes.

Questions
- **What is the worst sin you can think of? What sin is the least offensive?**
- **What makes the two sins so different?**
  Read 1 John 3:4.

- **How can God see all sin the same?**
- **How does this affect your view of sin?**
- **How should you treat people who have "big" sins in their past?**

SIN—The Gentle Slope Down

Title: THE LION KING (G)

Scripture: Galatians 5:7-10

Alternate Takes: Prodigal Son (Luke 15:11-32),
Rejecting God (Jeremiah 8:9),
Salvation (Luke 23:39-43)

START TIME: *1 hour, 6 minutes, 15 seconds*
START CUE: *Simba talks to Rafiki.*
END TIME: *1 hour, 8 minutes, 15 seconds*
END CUE: *Simba runs away.*
DURATION: *2 minutes*

Overview: Simba confesses that he's lost his way. He began as the son of the lion king, but now he's miles away with no clue as to how he got there. Mufasa, his father, appears in a vision and challenges him to remember and return to his heritage. Simba can overcome his past by learning from his mistakes.

Illustration: Sin rarely swoops in and tackles us in an instant. Instead, it gradually weasels its way into our attitudes and actions, and over a lifetime it leads us to a place far from where we intended to be. Thankfully, God never leaves us, and he always calls us to return.

Questions

- **Have you ever asked yourself, "How did I get here?" When?**
- **Were you able to get back to where you needed to be?**
  Read Galatians 5:7-10.
- **What are some "yeast" sins?**
- **How can you guard yourself against sins that grow over the years?**
- **Is there a small sin in your life now that could become huge in the future? What will you do about it?**

SIN NATURE—Jekyll & Hyde

Title: WILLIAM SHAKESPEARE'S
ROMEO + JULIET (PG-13)

Scripture: Romans 7:14-21

Alternate Takes: Possessions (Isaiah 44:13-17),
Taming the Tongue (James 3:8)

START TIME: *45 minutes, 30 seconds*
START CUE: *Father Laurence shows a flower to some kids.*
END TIME: *46 minutes, 45 seconds*
END CUE: *Romeo interrupts Father Laurence.*
DURATION: *1 minute, 15 seconds*

Overview: Father Laurence surveys his garden and explains the dual nature of plants—that death and beauty can reside in the same flower.

Illustration: Who would have guessed that a brief horticulture lesson in a DiCaprio flick could perfectly illustrate man's sin nature?! Each of us can do good one minute and evil the next. Following Christ makes us alive, while reverting to old sin patterns brings death. This floral analogy makes this thorny (puns still live!) issue easier to understand.

Questions

- **Are any of you allergic to something that can kill you or make you sick? What is it?**
- **What things other than plants can be both beautiful and deadly?**
  Read Romans 7:14-21.
- **Can you relate to Paul? How is our spiritual life like the flowers in the film clip?**
- **Will we ever stop sinning? Why or why not?**
- **What can you do to be beautiful and not poisonous?**

SPIRIT WORLD—Do You Believe in Ghosts?

Title: THE SIXTH SENSE (PG-13)

Scripture: Daniel 10:4-14

Alternate Takes: Spiritual Blindness (Ephesians 2:1-2),
Afterlife (1 Corinthians 15:50-57)

START TIME: *50 minutes, 00 seconds*
START CUE: *Cole says he's ready to tell his secret.*
END TIME: *51 minutes, 15 seconds*
END CUE: *Cole tries to go to sleep.*
DURATION: *1 minute, 15 seconds*

Overview: Cole finally reveals his secret to Dr. Crowe—that he sees dead people. Cole's sixth sense enables him to see dead people walking around like normal people. These ghosts wander the earth with no idea about their true condition.

Illustration: The issue of the spiritual world is hot right now, and you should be applying the Bible to the hype. So much of what people believe comes from movies and their parents. Use this hugely popular film to apply biblical ideas to teens' views about spirits and the afterlife.

Questions
- **Have any of you had what you believe to be a supernatural experience? What happened?**
- **Do you believe in ghosts and spirits? Why or why not?**
  Read Daniel 10:4-14.
- **What details about the spiritual world can you find in this passage about battling angels? According to verse 12, what was Daniel's role in the angel's actions?**
- **How does this passage make you feel about the spiritual world?**
- **In what ways can the spiritual world affect your physical life? How will you respond?**

SPIRITUAL BLINDNESS—The Big Secret

Title: THE TRUMAN SHOW (PG)

Scripture: 2 Corinthians 4:4

Alternate Take: Seeking God (Matthew 7:7)

START TIME: *14 minutes, 45 seconds*
START CUE: *Truman thinks he sees his dad.*
END TIME: *16 minutes, 00 seconds*
END CUE: *Truman is left alone in the street.*
DURATION: *1 minute, 45 seconds*

Overview: Truman thinks he sees his dead father on the street. When he attempts to talk to him, though, the entire world (buses, joggers, dogs, etc.) seemingly conspires against him and prevents him from talking to his dad and discovering the truth.

Illustration: This clip can be used to illustrate how Satan tries to keep people blind to the truth. He wants pre-believers to remain ignorant of their true spiritual state (separation from God). When people glimpse the truth, Satan throws everything in their way to distract them and prevent them from finding it.

Questions
- Have you ever felt like the world was trying to keep you from something? What?

  Read 2 Corinthians 4:4.
- How does Satan keep sinners blind to their spiritual slavery?
- Why doesn't God prevent Satan from blinding people?
- When and how did you learn about the truth of the gospel?
- How can you make it easier for people to see and hear the truth?

SPIRITUAL GROWTH—Practice Makes Perfect

Title: THE SANDLOT (PG)

Scripture: 2 Peter 3:17-18

Alternate Take: Focus (Proverbs 4:25-27)

START TIME: *11 minutes, 30 seconds*
START CUE: *Scotty and Bill exit the house.*
END TIME: *13 minutes, 00 seconds*
END CUE: *Scotty gets hit in the eye with the baseball.*
DURATION: *1 minute, 30 seconds*

Overview: Scotty goes into the backyard with his stepdad, Bill, to learn how to play catch. Bill tells Scotty to keep his eye on the ball. Scotty can't catch the ball or even throw it back to Bill. When Scotty finally does keep his eye on the ball, he gets a black eye.

Illustration: Sometimes we think accepting Christ brings an instant seminary degree with it. (All that school for nothing!) While the Holy Spirit does indwell us, lots of spiritual growth must take place. Once we discover God, we must spend time learning about him in order to know him intimately. (In other words, we need to move from the farm league to the majors.)

Questions
- What thing in your life have you had to work at the hardest to learn? Why did you stick with it?

  Read 2 Peter 3:17-18.
- What are some ways that we can grow in the grace and knowledge of God?
- Why doesn't God just zap you with everything you need to know about him?
- What is the most recent thing God has taught you and how have you changed because of it?
- What are some ways you can speed up your spiritual growth?

SPIRITUAL GROWTH—You're a Big Boy Now

Title: STAR WARS: EPISODE 1—
THE PHANTOM MENACE (PG)

Scripture: 1 Corinthians 3:1-7

Alternate Takes: Freedom (1 Corinthians 6:20),
God's Will (Matthew 10:37-39)

START TIME: *1 hour, 9 minutes, 00 seconds*
START CUE: *Qui-Gon and Anakin enter his house.*
END TIME: *1 hour, 11 minutes, 30 seconds*
END CUE: *Qui-Gon places his hand on Shmi's shoulder.*
DURATION: *2 minutes, 30 seconds*

Overview: Qui-Gon tells Anakin that he is free. Unfortunately, Anakin's mother is still a slave. Anakin doesn't want to leave Shmi, but she encourages him to follow the path set before him.

Illustration: We've all got to leave home at some time (and sometimes our parents even change the locks while we're gone). This idea of finding your own path is also true spiritually. Many people who grow up in the church have their parents' faith. They follow their parents' lead and imitate them. At some point, people each have to claim their faith for themselves, move out from under their parents' wing, and venture into a relationship with Christ alone. Use this clip to show kids that the transition may be scary, but the amazing thing about God is that he's interested in getting to know *each one of us.*

Questions

- **When was the first time you left home for a week away from your parents? How did you react?**
- **What are the physical differences between infants and adults? the emotional differences? the spiritual differences?**
  Read 1 Corinthians 3:1-7.
- **What do you think is the difference between spiritual milk and meat?**
- **How can you develop your own faith in Christ and not simply rely on what you parents or other people tell you?**
- **What needs to happen for you to move from spiritual milk to solid food?**

STEWARDSHIP—Where Does It Go?

Title: DAVE (PG-13)

Scripture: Luke 16:10-13

Alternate Take: Compassion (1 Peter 3:8-9)

START TIME: *56 minutes, 00 seconds*
START CUE: *Dave says he's found a way to save the homeless shelters.*
END TIME: *59 minutes, 00 seconds*
END CUE: *Dave says, "We're doing real good!"*
DURATION: *3 minutes*

Overview: Dave wants to find a way to cut the federal budget by $650 million so the money can be used to fund homeless shelters. He asks his colleagues where they can cut money from their bloated budgets in order to help real people with real problems.

Illustration: Those old souvenirs always seem to shout, "What were you *thinking?*" (You don't believe me? Just look at that Statue of Liberty-shaped pecan log one more time.) Sometimes we aren't the best stewards of our money. Instead of using what God blesses us with to help others and meet needs, we get that eighth pair of jeans we absolutely *must* have. Becoming a good steward takes time and discipline, but God rewards the sacrifice with even greater responsibility.

Questions
- **What is the most recent thing you wasted your money on?**
- **Why did you buy it?**
- **What would have been a better use of that money?**
  Read Luke 16:10-13.
- **What does stewardship mean?**
- **How can you start using your money and possessions for God's kingdom and not just for yourself?**

SUBSTANCE ABUSE—You Look SO Cool

Title: THE SANDLOT (PG)

Scripture: Proverbs 23:29-35

Alternate Take: Peer Pressure (Proverbs 2:20-22)

START TIME: *49 minutes, 30 seconds*
START CUE: *The Kid holds up a bag of chewing tobacco.*
END TIME: *52 minutes, 30 seconds*
END CUE: *The team exits the ride covered in vomit.*
DURATION: *3 minutes*

Overview: All of the guys take a plug of chewing tobacco before they get on the amusement park ride. Their fun disappears, though, when the tobacco makes them sick, and they spend the ride vomiting.

Illustration: If you can stomach this scene (it's pretty gross), it makes a great way to start a discussion. The point is obvious: Substance abuse may be fun in the beginning, but sooner or later, it'll make you look stupid and feel terrible.

Questions

- Have you ever had an experience similar to the one in this scene? What did you learn?
- Why do you think people use addictive substances?
- Where do you stand when it comes to drugs and alcohol? Do you think using drugs and alcohol is a big deal? Why or why not?
   Read Proverbs 23:29-35.
- What are the physical and spiritual consequences of using drugs and alcohol?
- What do you think of people who get involved with addictive substances? How can you reach out to them?

SUCCESS—Jesus Is for Losers

Title: DROP DEAD GORGEOUS (PG-13)

Scripture: Exodus 20:7

Alternate Takes: Work (1 Corinthians 10:31), Salvation (Matthew 16:25)

START TIME: *8 minutes, 30 seconds*
START CUE: *Becky Leeman fires at a target.*
END TIME: *9 minutes, 00 seconds*
END CUE: *Becky aims her gun.*
DURATION: *30 seconds*

Overview: Becky, the front-running beauty contestant, demonstrates her talents on the firing range. She recounts receiving her gun as a Christmas present with a card reading "Jesus loves winners."

Illustration: God doesn't care who wins the Super Bowl (although I know he prefers the Cowboys). Many people misinterpret allegiance to God as a divine mandate to win and to live an earthly life of material abundance. This is not true, and the clip helps show how absurd this attitude is. Jesus loves everyone, and he came because we are all *losers* who need his saving grace.

Questions

- When have you seen people bringing God into competitions? How do you feel about that?
   Read Exodus 20:7.
- How does Becky use the Lord's name in vain?

- Does Jesus love winners more than he loves other people? Why or why not?
- Can we earn God's affection through success? Do you ever struggle with trying to earn God's love?
- In what areas of your life do you need to stop trying to use God for personal gain?

TALENTS—Everybody's Got One

Title: EDWARD SCISSORHANDS (PG-13)

Scripture: Matthew 25:14-30

Alternate Take: Encouragement (Ephesians 2:19-22)

START TIME: *45 minutes, 00 seconds*
START CUE: *Edward stands at the front of the class for Show and Tell.*
END TIME: *45 minutes, 30 seconds*
END CUE: *Edward displays his handiwork to the class.*
DURATION: *30 seconds*

Overview: Edward stands in front of the class for Show and Tell. He takes a piece of paper and, with his scissor-hands, makes an amazing paper cutout.

Illustration: Everybody has a talent! God made us all different, with different gifts, so that we could use our talents to expand the kingdom of God. To hide your gift or use it for selfish gain is sin. Use this Scripture passage about talents (coins) to talk about how your kids can use their talents (abilities) to serve the Lord.

Questions
- What is your best talent?
- How do you hope to use your talent in the future?
  Read Matthew 25:14-30.
- What does this parable mean?
- How have you begun to use the talents God has entrusted to you?
- How can you glorify God with these talents?

TAMING THE TONGUE—Cuts Like a Knife

Title: EMMA (PG)

Scripture: James 3:3-12

Alternate Take: Pride (Philippians 2:3-5)

START TIME: *1 hour, 29 minutes, 15 seconds*
START CUE: *Miss Bates jokes that she always has dull things to say.*
END TIME: *1 hour, 30 minutes, 45 seconds*
END CUE: *Miss Bates and Mr. Knightley leave.*
DURATION: *1 minute, 30 seconds*

Overview: Miss Bates jokes that she will be able to win the game they're playing by saying three dull things. Emma responds that it will be difficult for her to limit her dull comments to only three.

Illustration: This scene is realistically harsh and should help everyone understand what it feels like to be cut to the quick. Words are incredibly powerful! Try to imagine a world in which people put their energy into building everyone up instead of thinking of witty comebacks. It's hard to imagine, but possible to achieve, if we start choosing our words carefully. Use this clip to help your students evaluate the way they speak to each other.

Questions
- **How did this clip make you feel?**
- **How do you react when someone cuts you down?**
  Read James 3:3-12.
- **Does this passage mean put-downs are a sin? Why or why not?**
- **How would your life and your relationships change if you spoke only words of encouragement?**
- **How can you keep your tongue from cutting other people down?**

TAMING THE TONGUE—I'm Rubber, You're Glue

Title: MONTY PYTHON AND THE HOLY GRAIL (PG)

Scripture: 1 Thessalonians 5:11

Alternate Take: Hospitality (Romans 12:10-14)

START TIME: *26 minutes, 00 seconds*
START CUE: *Arthur and his knights stop at a castle wall.*
END TIME: *28 minutes, 15 seconds*
END CUE: *The castle guard sticks out his tongue at them.*
DURATION: *2 minutes, 15 seconds*

Themes

R-Z

Overview: King Arthur and his knights approach a castle and ask for information about the Holy Grail. The guard taunts them mercilessly, calling them all sorts of silly names, and he refuses to let them in the castle.

Illustration: Admit it—you've used similar phrases behind your senior pastor's back. Since the first words that come to mind in difficult situations are generally put-downs and smart remarks, taming the tongue is especially difficult. This scene provides a silly start to a serious discussion.

Questions
- **Have you ever insulted someone before? What happened?**
- **Have you ever been insulted? How did it make you feel?**
  Read 1 Thessalonians 5:11.
- **Why is it so hard to speak only encouraging words? How does encouragement affect other people?**
- **What are some practical ways you can learn restraint when you're tempted to say rude or mean things?**
- **What will you have to do to change your put-downs into words of encouragement?**

THANKFULNESS—You Shouldn't Have

Title: THE MUPPET CHRISTMAS CAROL (G)

Scripture: 1 Thessalonians 5:16-18

Alternate Takes: Contentment (2 Corinthians 12:9-10), Bless Your Enemies (Luke 6:27-28)

START TIME: *59 minutes, 00 seconds*
START CUE: *The Cratchit family sits at the table.*
END TIME: *1 hour, 00 minutes, 45 seconds*
END CUE: *Tiny Tim says, "God bless us every one."*
DURATION: *1 minute, 45 seconds*

Overview: Kermit (as Mr. Cratchit) sits with his family at the dinner table and thanks Mr. Scrooge for the meal. Miss Piggy takes exception to this, since Scrooge keeps them in near poverty. Tiny Tim, crutches and all, agrees with his dad and is thankful for all his blessings.

Illustration: I sometimes think Paul made a mistake when he said to always be thankful. (He never paid taxes to Uncle Sam!) It's in the Bible, though, which means it's true. This scene shows God's desire being lived out by folks who are thankful for the meager things they do have.

Questions

- Who do you relate to in the clip? Why?
- How can Tiny Tim be thankful when he's crippled? How would you feel if you were in a situation similar to his?
- How do people you know who have experienced tragedy remain positive and thankful?

  Read 1 Thessalonians 5:16-18.

- Why is it so hard to "give thanks in all circumstances"?
- What are some situations you are not thankful for? How can you be thankful for them?

TRAGEDY—Why Do Bad Things Happen?

Title: PATCH ADAMS (PG-13)

Scripture: James 1:13-15

Alternate Takes: God in Nature (Psalm 19:1-6), Questioning God (Matthew 7:7)

START TIME: *1 hour, 32 minutes, 15 seconds*
START CUE: *Patch stands at the edge of a cliff.*
END TIME: *1 hour, 34 minutes, 45 seconds*
END CUE: *The butterfly flies away.*
DURATION: *2 minutes, 30 seconds*

Overview: Patch Adams questions God after the murder of his girlfriend and blames him for the lack of compassion in the world. God answers Patch through a delicate butterfly. Patch smiles and realizes that there is good in the world and that the Creator does care. Life, unfortunately, must contain pain and suffering in the midst of beauty.

Illustration: This scene asks non-Christians' most popular question: If God exists, why is there so much pain? Ironically, an atheist's approach to this question will still provide the correct answer. When someone doesn't believe in God, the blame for the world's ills lands on the only possible cause—humanity. God does exist, though, and things would be much worse without him. Use this clip to kick-start a brainstorming session on the difficult topic of faith in the midst of tragedy.

Questions

- What did the butterfly mean?
- Have you experienced a tragedy? What happened?

- **Why do people blame God for tragedies?**
  Read James 1:13-15.
- **What is the source of pain and evil on earth?**
- **How can you show God's love to others who are in the midst of a tragedy?**

TRIALS—What Doesn't Kill You...

Title: JAWS (PG-13)

Scripture: 1 Peter 1:6-9

Alternate Takes: Emotional Scars (Psalm 147:3), Confession (James 5:16)

START TIME: *1 hour, 26 minutes, 30 seconds*
START CUE: *Hooper asks Quint where he got his scar.*
END TIME: *1 hour, 28 minutes, 00 seconds*
END CUE: *Quint and Hooper laugh at their scars.*
DURATION: *1 minute, 30 seconds*

Overview: Quint and Hooper show each other their scars, one-upping each other's stories about how they received them.

Illustration: All of us have scars—both physical and emotional—that we've received from the trials in our lives. God uses these difficult times to mold our faith and to make us strong. Though they hurt for a time, they perfect us and turn us into images of Christ.

Questions
- **What is the worst physical injury or scar you have gotten?**
- **How are physical scars and emotional scars different? Which is worse?**
  Read 1 Peter 1:6-9.
- **Is God the one who sends trials upon us? Why or why not?**
- **What other promises does God make that can help you through trials?**
- **What are some ways we can help each other through difficult times in the future?**

TRUST—Built on Trust?

Title: SOME KIND OF WONDERFUL (PG-13)

Scripture: Psalm 40:4

Alternate Take: Integrity (Proverbs 12:19-20)

START TIME: *12 minutes, 45 seconds*
START CUE: *Keith works on a painting.*
END TIME: *14 minutes, 15 seconds*
END CUE: *Amanda looks at her new ring.*
DURATION: *1 minute, 30 seconds*

Overview: Hardy tells his "side dish" that relationships are all built on trust. His girlfriend Amanda catches him cheating, but he explains the indiscretion away and says that he trusts Amanda because that's what their relationship is built on.

Illustration: Never trust a person who dresses like someone on *Miami Vice*, that's my motto. Relationships should be built on trust, but the danger is that you open yourself up to getting hurt. Trust must be earned and maintained. Thankfully you can trust God completely, because he will never cheat on you.

Questions
• **What does it take for someone to gain your trust?**
• **Have you ever been lied to? How did it feel?**
• **Can you ever trust that person again? Why or why not?**
   Read Psalm 40:4.
• **How has God earned your trust? What blessings do we receive from trusting God?**
• **How can you become more trustworthy?**

TRUST—But I Trusted You!

Title: SAY ANYTHING (PG-13)

Scripture: Jeremiah 17:5-7

Alternate Takes: Parents (Exodus 20:12),
Rationalizing Sin (Titus 1:15-16),
Stealing (Exodus 20:15)

START TIME: *1 hour, 21 minutes, 30 seconds*
START CUE: *Diane walks into the kitchen to talk to her father.*
END TIME: *1 hour, 24 minutes, 00 seconds*
END CUE: *Diane exits the kitchen.*
DURATION: *2 minutes, 30 seconds*

Overview: Mr. Court, Diane's father, vehemently denies the IRS's accusations that he is a thief. Diane confronts him with the money she found hidden in the house and catches him in his lie. He justifies his crime, claiming he did it all for her, and destroys her faith in him.

Illustration: Unfortunately, the people we love and trust will fail us at some point. Placing total trust and faith in people here on earth only causes disillusionment and disappointment. God, however, succeeds where all of humanity fails. He knows us and loves us intimately, and he never fails to follow through on his promises.

Questions
- **Have your parents ever failed you? How?**
- **Have you forgiven them?**
  Read Jeremiah 17:5-7.
- **Why can we put our complete trust in God?**
- **How have you trusted God? What happened?**
- **How can you keep trusting God even when he seems to fail you?**

TRUTH—How Do I Look?

Title: LIAR LIAR (PG-13)

Scripture: John 17:17-19

Alternate Take: Lying (Proverbs 13:5; Proverbs 28:23)

START TIME: *38 minutes, 30 seconds*
START CUE: *Fletcher walks onto the playground with his son.*
END TIME: *40 minutes, 00 seconds*
END CUE: *Max agrees to try and undo his wish.*
DURATION: *1 minute, 30 seconds*

Overview: Fletcher (a lawyer) begs his son, Max, to take back the magical birthday wish that forces Fletcher to tell only the truth. Fletcher explains that adults have to lie—it's just a normal part of life that Max will understand some day.

Illustration: Fletcher says what most people think today: Truth is negotiable and depends on the circumstances. God isn't so "enlightened." He *is* truth and calls us to live in truth also. Though lies may fix short-term problems, they always eventually unravel and make things many times worse.

Questions
- **What is the last white lie you told?**
- **Are lies wrong? When do you feel tempted to tell lies?**
  Read John 17:17-19.

- What do you think it means to be sanctified by the truth? How should we live out this idea?
- Is it possible to always tell the truth? Why or why not?
- How would living by truth change your daily life?

TRUTH—It Looks True From Here

Title: RETURN OF THE JEDI (PG)

Scripture: John 8:31-32

Alternate Takes: Confession (Proverbs 28:13), Parents (Exodus 34:6-7)

START TIME: *45 minutes, 00 seconds*
START CUE: *Obi-Wan Kenobi makes a ghostly appearance.*
END TIME: *45 minutes, 45 seconds*
END CUE: *Yoda appears.*
DURATION: *45 seconds*

Overview: Luke asks Obi-Wan Kenobi why he didn't tell him the truth—that Darth Vader is his father. Obi-Wan rationalizes that he told the truth from a certain perspective since all things are true when viewed from different angles.

Illustration: Obi-Wan may present the world's view of truth, but it's not God's. Popular opinion would have us believe that truth is relative to where people are and how they see it. God, however, gave us an absolute standard for truth—everything that is consistent with his character and God's Word is true in all situations for all people and at all times. (Not much room for white lies, is there?)

Questions
- Is Obi-Wan correct about the nature of truth? Why or why not?
- Are white lies ever OK? Why or why not?
  Read John 8:31-32.
- What does the truth set us free from?
- Why does God care so much about truth?
- How can you live with God's truth in your everyday life?

TRUTH—My Other Car Is a Lexus

Title: BIG DADDY (PG-13)

Scripture: Ephesians 4:25

Alternate Takes: Pride (Proverbs 29:23), Contentment (Psalm 139:14-16)

START TIME: *45 minutes, 15 seconds*
START CUE: *Sonny and his date enter his living room.*
END TIME: *46 minutes, 00 seconds*
END CUE: *Sonny confesses to lying.*
DURATION: *45 seconds*

Overview: Sonny attempts to impress his date. She mentions that she loves the band STYX, and he makes up stories about his experiences with the band so that she will like him.

Illustration: We all put on our best face for dates (unless you're Brad Pitt, 'cause a face like his covers many sins). Though Sonny admits he is lying, the scene points out how common it is to lie to impress a date. People typically put on a show—saying the right things, dressing the right way, and going to the right places—for the person they like, keeping the real deal hidden for a few months.

Questions
- **Have you ever made up a story to impress a date? What happened?**
- **Have you ever thought you knew someone and later discovered that he or she was different? What happened?**
- **Why do we try to impress people?**
  Read Ephesians 4:25.
- **Why is honesty the best policy in dating relationships?**
- **How can you develop the confidence to be yourself?**

TRUTH—You Say Potato...

Title: SO I MARRIED AN AXE MURDERER (PG-13)

Scripture: Psalm 31:1-5

Alternate Takes: Hate (Matthew 5:21-22),
Murder (Exodus 20:13)

START TIME: *21 minutes, 15 seconds*
START CUE: *Charlie and Harriet walk up to the bay.*
END TIME: *22 minutes, 15 seconds*
END CUE: *Charlie looks uncomfortable.*
DURATION: *1 minute*

Overview: Charlie asks Harriet if she has ever brutally murdered someone. She responds that what may be brutal to one person might be reasonable to another.

Illustration: Today truth is so relative and changes constantly from person to person in the name of tolerance. God's truth, however, is eternal and applies to everyone at all times. This scene's extreme example of relativism will open teens' minds to the need for absolute truth.

Questions
- **What is the most bizarre thing anyone has ever told you?**
- **Do your friends at school believe there are definite rights and wrongs? Why or why not?**
  Read Psalm 31:1-5.
- **According to verse 5, why can we turn to God's Word for standards for living?**
- **How do you deal with people who do not believe God's truth?**
- **What current situation do you need to apply God's absolute truth to?**

UNITY—Strength in Numbers

Title: A BUG'S LIFE (G)

Scripture: 1 Corinthians 12:25-27

Alternate Take: Persistence (Luke 18:1-8)

START TIME: *55 minutes, 00 seconds*
START CUE: *Hopper's goons ask him to forget the ants.*
END TIME: *56 minutes, 30 seconds*
END CUE: *Hopper and his gang fly away.*
DURATION: *1 minute, 30 seconds*

Overview: Hopper explains to his gang that one ant may be harmless and unable to stop them, like throwing one seed at a gang member. Hundreds of ants joined together, though, could bury them as surely as hundreds of seeds do. This speech (and demonstration) rallies his gang to crush the ants' spirit before they can rise up.

Illustration: Christians sometimes think they can't change the world. We ask, "What can one person do?" Yet a timid Christian voice can become a roar when that voice joins together with the voices of others in a congregation and the voices of the entire body of Christ. We will only truly impact the world by joining forces with other believers. The mission of a coordinated body of Christ can change the world on an unimaginable scale.

Questions
- **How is Hopper like a non-Christian and the seeds/ants like Christians?**
  Read 1 Corinthians 12:25-27.
- **Can anything stop the united body of Christ?**
- **What types of things keep Christians from joining together?**

- What causes can the church rally around?
- How can you help create unity between all Christians?

WITNESSING–Save Yourself!

Title: TITANIC (PG-13)

Scripture: Acts 1:8

Alternate Take: Boldness (Acts 9:28-29)

START TIME: *1 hour, 17 minutes, 45 seconds*
START CUE: *Jack gets Rose alone.*
END TIME: *1 hour, 19 minutes, 30 seconds*
END CUE: *Rose leaves Jack.*
DURATION: *1 minute, 45 seconds*

Overview: Jack confronts Rose about her impending marriage to Cal. He states that by staying with Cal, the light and fire within her will be snuffed out. He desperately wants to rescue Rose from her plight, but he realizes that only she can decide to save herself.

Illustration: I wish I didn't relate to this clip so well. (No, not being stuck on a sinking ship, although being a Dallas Mavericks fan is something like that.) I wish there was a way to make pre-believers know the truth of the gospel, but only they can make a decision to accept freedom in Christ. Though Jack approaches Rose out of romantic love, the emotions are the same when we approach someone out of spiritual love. This scene will prompt teenagers to consider how they relate to those who don't know Jesus.

Questions
- **What is the spark that Jack is talking about, and why can only Rose save herself?**
  Read Acts 1:8.
- **How is this scene like witnessing?**
- **What are some ways to show people the truth of the life they're leading without Christ?**
- **How should you treat a person who rejects salvation?**
- **Who can you pray for and witness to in your life?**

WITNESSING—By Any Means Necessary

Title: MR. HOLLAND'S OPUS (PG)

Scripture: 1 Corinthians 9:19-23

Alternate Takes: Conflict (Matthew 12:9-14), Music (Ephesians 5:19-20)

START TIME: *41 minutes, 15 seconds*
START CUE: *Gene says Mr. Holland is teaching rock-and-roll.*
END TIME: *42 minutes, 45 seconds*
END CUE: *Mrs. Jacobs says, "I can tell them that."*
DURATION: *1 minute, 30 seconds*

Overview: The principal and vice principal question Mr. Holland's use of rock music in his music appreciation class. Mr. Holland defends his teaching methods and says he will use whatever music he can to teach his students to love music.

Illustration: Bet this scene felt familiar, huh? It's like trying to defend the punk show you put on in the sanctuary! People often question what they don't understand, and that includes methods of sharing the gospel. Use this clip to let your students know that, as campus missionaries, they should use whatever means possible to connect the gospel to hurt and lost people.

Questions
- **What current fad or style do your parents not understand?**
- **Why do you think they don't like it?**
    Read 1 Corinthians 9:19-23.
- **How was the movie clip similar to what Paul said about sharing the gospel?**
- **Does God give us a right and wrong way to share the gospel? Explain.**
- **What fresh and unusual ways can you use to share the good news with others in your school?**

WITNESSING—Do You See What I See?

Title: CONTACT (PG)

Scripture: John 9:24-34

Alternate Take: Standing Firm (2 Thessalonians 2:15-17)

START TIME: *2 hours, 13 minutes, 15 seconds*
START CUE: *Ellie testifies before a Senate committee.*
END TIME: *2 hours, 16 minutes, 00 seconds*
END CUE: *Ellie refuses to deny her testimony.*
DURATION: *2 minutes, 45 seconds*

Overview: Ellie testifies that she made contact with aliens. The Senate committee won't believe her without proof. Ellie says that she wishes everyone could see what she saw because then people wouldn't deny what she experienced.

Illustration: This sounds like a desperate plea with pre-believers—"If only you could feel Jesus like I do!" That's the problem: People can't experience Jesus through you, they must experience Jesus for themselves. We must press forward, though, and try to convey the joy and beauty of the grace we experience, even if we have no physical evidence.

Questions
- **When has something happened to you that no one believed? What happened?**
- **How did you get people to believe you?**
  Read John 9:24-34.
- **How is sharing your faith like the man telling the Pharisees he was healed?**
- **What things keep people from seeing what you see and believing what you have experienced?**
- **How can you make God more real to people?**

WITNESSING—Why Didn't You Tell Me?!

Title: JAWS (PG-13)

Scripture: 1 Peter 5:8

Alternate Takes: Forgiveness (Genesis 50:17), Knowledge (James 4:17)

START TIME: *36 minutes, 00 seconds*
START CUE: *A grieving mother approaches Brody.*
END TIME: *37 minutes, 30 seconds*
END CUE: *The mother leaves a stunned Brody.*
DURATION: *1 minute, 30 seconds*

Overview: A mother slaps police chief Brody after the funeral of her only son. She asks him why he allowed people to swim when he knew a killer shark was in the waters.

Illustration: We would warn our friends not to swim in shark-infested waters. Yet we often overlook our friends' spiritual peril. We must alert people to the danger of eternal separation from God before it's too late, so they will never ask us, "Why didn't you tell me?"

Questions

• **What would you have said to Brody if your brother or sister had been killed by the shark?**

   Read 1 Peter 5:8.

• **How is Satan like Jaws?**

• **What keeps you from telling your friends about their spiritual danger?**

• **What are different ways you can share the gospel with your friends?**

• **Who can you share the gospel with this week?**

Movie Background Index

★　　　★　　　★

Aladdin discovers the magic lamp that turns him from a street urchin into a prince. With the help of the Genie (Robin Williams) and his friends, he fights Jafar for the safety of the kingdom and the love of Princess Jasmine.

Salieri (F. Murray Abraham) recounts his life as teacher to musical genius and social deviant Wolfgang Amadeus Mozart (Tom Hulce). Salieri's love of God and music turns to jealousy and eventually to utter hatred because of Mozart.

Based on the true story of the amazing rescue of the Apollo 13 astronauts. Jim Lovell (Tom Hanks), Fred Haise (Bill Paxton), and Jack Swigert's (Kevin Bacon) mission to the moon gets cut short by an outer space explosion, and they must work together with NASA to get back to earth.

Sixties super spy and fashion photographer Austin Powers (Mike Myers) is unfrozen in the nineties. He joins agent Vanessa Kensington (Elizabeth Hurley) in stopping Dr. Evil's plan to hold the world hostage with the threat of a nuclear bomb.

Austin Powers (Mike Myers) returns to foil Dr. Evil's diabolical plans to rule the world. This time, Austin goes back in time to recover his stolen "mojo" and to stop Dr. Evil from using a laser on the moon to blow up Washington, D.C.

BATMAN FOREVER (PG-13) Warner Bros., 1995 . . . . **111**
Batman (Val Kilmer) and Robin (Chris O'Donnell) must stop The Riddler (Jim Carrey) and Two-Face's (Tommy Lee Jones) plan to rule Gotham City with a device that drains people's brains into their TV sets.

BEAUTY AND THE BEAST (G)
Walt Disney Productions, 1991 . . . . **79, 111**
Belle, the beautiful girl who loves books, becomes the prisoner in the castle of the Beast, where they both learn to laugh and love one another.

BETTER OFF DEAD (PG) 20th Century Fox, 1985 . . . . **36**
Lane Myer (John Cusack) plays a suicidal teen who cannot get over his girlfriend's breaking up with him. (Though it talks about a dark subject, the film is absurdly hysterical with a broad *Airplane!*-style humor.)

BIG DADDY (PG-13) Columbia Pictures, 1999 . . . . **92, 131**
Sonny Koufax (Adam Sandler) lives a childish, immature, slacker life. He finds an abandoned child on his doorstep, and learns responsibility and the joys of family.

A BUG'S LIFE (G) Walt Disney Productions, 1998 . . . . **46, 86, 133**
Flik, a misunderstood dreamer, leaves his ant colony to find help against Hopper and his oppressive gang of grasshoppers. Flik returns with a band of circus performer bugs that he passes off as warriors. When the charade crumbles, the ants must overcome their fears and traditions to win their freedom.

CAN'T HARDLY WAIT (PG-13) Columbia Pictures, 1998 . . . . . **63, 82, 114**
This movie highlights the various trials and victories of seniors Amanda (Jennifer Love Hewitt), Preston (Ethan Embry), William (Charlie Korsmo), Denise (Lauren Ambrose), and Kenny (Seth Green) at their graduation night party.

CONTACT (PG) Warner Bros., 1997 . . . . **58, 135**
Dr. Eleanor Arroway (Jodie Foster) devoted her life to the search for extraterrestrial life. She finds it in a message from outer space that contains the plans to a spaceship, and she fights for the right to be the one who contacts the aliens.

DAVE (PG-13) Warner Bros., 1993 . . . . **15, 121**
Dave Kovic (Kevin Kline) does the greatest Presidential impersonation in history when he must fill in for the real U.S. President, who is incapacitated with a stroke. Dave turns Washington upside down when he applies his down-home integrity to politics.

Movie Background Index

FORREST GUMP (PG-13) Paramount Pictures, 1994 . . . . **52, 73, 84**
Forrest Gump (Tom Hanks) is a dimwitted man with a large heart and a charmed life. Through dumb luck and clean living, Forrest touches everyone he meets on his way through an extraordinary life.

THE FRESHMAN (PG) TriStar Pictures, 1990 . . . . **113**
Clark Kellogg (Matthew Broderick), a college freshman and brand new resident of New York City, finds himself in the middle of Carmine Sabatini's (Marlon Brando) mob family and a huge ring of exotic animal smugglers.

GALAXY QUEST (PG) DreamWorks SKG, 1999 . . . . **25, 77**
Commander Taggart (Tim Allen) and the rest of the crew of the canceled TV show *Galaxy Quest* (including Sigourney Weaver and Alan Rickman) find themselves out of science fiction conventions and in space, fighting for the freedom of the alien Thermians who think the *Galaxy Quest* show was historical fact, not entertainment.

GROUNDHOG DAY (PG) Columbia Pictures, 1993 . . . . **17**
Phil Connors (Bill Murray) finds himself reliving the same day (Groundhog Day) over and over and over until he learns to care for others, not just himself.

HAPPY GILMORE (PG-13) Universal Pictures, 1996 . . . . **24, 25**
Happy Gilmore (Adam Sandler) is a hockey player turned golfer with a huge swing and an enormous temper. He must learn to curb his anger and pride in order to win enough money to save his grandmother's house.

HOOSIERS (PG) Orion Pictures, 1986 . . . . **99**
This film depicts the inspiring true story of a small-town Indiana basketball team that goes all the way to the state basketball finals.

HOPE FLOATS (PG-13) 20th Century Fox, 1998 . . . . **19, 42, 91**
Birdee's (Sandra Bullock) world falls apart when she discovers her husband is cheating on her. She returns to her childhood home in Texas with her young daughter Bernice to start over and discover herself.

INDIANA JONES AND THE LAST CRUSADE (PG-13)
Paramount Pictures, 1989 . . . . **49, 66, 97**
Indiana Jones (Harrison Ford) must save his father (Sean Connery) and endure increasingly dangerous situations so they can find the Holy Grail before the Nazis do.

JAWS (PG-13) Universal Pictures, 1975 . . . . **128, 136**
Police chief Brody (Roy Scheider) and Dr. Hooper (Richard Dreyfuss) must find and kill a great white shark that terrorizes a small tourist town over a holiday weekend.

LIAR LIAR (PG-13) Universal Pictures, 1997 . . . . **130**
Fletcher Reede (Jim Carrey) is a smooth-talking lawyer who will lie about anything to win a case, until his son makes a wish that magically prohibits Fletcher from lying for 24 hours.

THE LION KING (G) Walt Disney Productions, 1994 . . . . **66, 70, 117**
Simba runs away from home, believing he is responsible for his father's death. The real killer, his evil uncle Scar, takes over the throne and ravages the once beautiful Pride Rock. Simba takes up a carefree lifestyle until his childhood friend Rafiki finds him and asks him to return and save Pride Rock.

THE LITTLE MERMAID (G)
Walt Disney Productions, 1989 . . . . **16**
Ariel, a mermaid, wants to be a human so she can be with Prince Eric. She gets her wish when evil Ursula makes a deal with her: Eric must kiss her within three days or Ariel will become Ursula's slave.

THE MAN WHO KNEW TOO LITTLE (PG)
Warner Bros., 1997. . . . . **90**
Wally Ritchie (Bill Murray) thinks he's pretending to be a spy in an elaborate "theater of life" production. In actuality, he has become involved in real-life intrigue, bumbling his way to becoming a super spy.

THE MASK (PG-13) New Line Cinema, 1994 . . . . **72, 84**
Stanley Ipkiss (Jim Carrey), a mild-mannered bank employee, discovers an ancient mask that, when worn, turns him into a cartoonish, mischievous superhero who ultimately saves the city and wins the girl through his outrageous antics.

THE MISSION (PG) Warner Bros., 1986 . . . . **40, 108, 115**
The Portuguese want to take over a Jesuit mission to the natives of the Brazilian rainforest so they can enslave the people. The peace-loving missionaries, led by Mendoza (Robert De Niro), join with their converts to defend themselves against the invasion.

MR. HOLLAND'S OPUS (PG) Hollywood Pictures, 1995 . . 23, 50, 96, 135

Mr. Holland (Richard Dreyfuss) puts aside his own ambitions in order to teach high school students to love music, impacting their lives forever.

MONTY PYTHON AND THE HOLY GRAIL (PG)
Python (Monty) Pictures, 1975 . . . . 16, 78, 125

The British comedy troupe sends up Camelot, King Arthur and the Knights of the Round Table with this bizarre and hysterical search for the Holy Grail.

THE MUPPET CHRISTMAS CAROL (G)
Walt Disney Productions, 1992 . . . . 58, 126

The Muppets redo the classic tale of the miser Ebenezer Scrooge (Michael Caine) and his encounters with the ghosts of Christmas past, present, and future.

THE MUPPET MOVIE (G) ITC Films, 1979 . . . . 69, 76

Kermit the Frog heads to Hollywood to make people happy. He gathers a crew of friends along the way, as well as the obsession of Doc Hopper who wants him to become the spokesman for his chain of frog-leg restaurants.

MUPPET TREASURE ISLAND (G)
Walt Disney Productions, 1996 . . . . 13, 39, 104

The Muppets redo the classic tale of young Jim and his fight to find the buried treasure before Long John Silver (Tim Curry) and his bloodthirsty pirates do.

NEVER BEEN KISSED (PG-13) 20th Century Fox, 1999. . . . . 36, 55

Josie Geller (Drew Barrymore), a journalist, goes undercover as a high school senior. While reliving high school, she learns about popularity, friendship, and love.

NINE MONTHS (PG-13) 20th Century Fox, 1995 18

Samuel (Hugh Grant) and Rebecca (Julianne Moore) are having their first baby. Samuel freaks out, but over the course of several misadventures, he finally discovers the joy of fatherhood.

NOTTING HILL (PG-13) Universal Pictures, 1999 . . . . 27, 43

Anna Scott (Julia Roberts), the most famous actress in the world, finds love with a bookstore owner, William (Hugh Grant), in this light romantic comedy.

Movie Background Index

REALITY BITES (PG-13) Universal Pictures, 1994 . . . . **102, 104, 114**

Lelaina (Winona Ryder) graduates as valedictorian of her university, but she can't find a job. She struggles along with her friends (including Ethan Hawke, Ben Stiller, and Janeane Garofalo) to find an identity, a job, and love in her new life in the "real world."

REAR WINDOW (PG) Universal Pictures, 1954 . . . . **82**

"Jeff" Jefferies (Jimmy Stewart), a photojournalist, watches his neighbors to pass the time while he's incapacitated by a broken leg. Intrigue ensues when he suspects one neighbor murdered his wife.

REBEL WITHOUT A CAUSE (NR) Warner Bros., 1955 . . . . **74**

Jim Stark (James Dean) is a confused youth seeking love, acceptance, and a nurturing family in middle-class America. Though released in 1955, this film (also starring Natalie Wood and Sal Mineo) still resonates today with themes and struggles common to twenty-first century teens.

RETURN OF THE JEDI (PG) 20th Century Fox, 1983. . . . . **109, 131**

The final chapter in the *Star Wars* saga wraps up all the loose ends of the series—freeing Han Solo (Harrison Ford) from captivity, resolving Luke's (Mark Hamill) questions and conflict with Darth Vader, and defeating the Emperor and his evil Empire.

RUNAWAY BRIDE (PG) Paramount Pictures, 1999 . . . . **51, 89, 116**

Maggie (Julia Roberts) has a problem with leaving fiancés at the altar—literally. Ike Graham (Richard Gere) is the reporter who comes to town to cover her next wedding, and he falls for the runaway bride.

THE SANDLOT (PG) 20th Century Fox, 1993 . . . . **62, 120, 122**

A group of kids spend the summer of '62 playing endless games of baseball. The game ends when they must rescue a baseball autographed by Babe Ruth from the clutches of a "demon" dog.

SAY ANYTHING (PG-13) 20th Century Fox, 1989 . . . . **54, 129**

Lloyd Dobler (John Cusack) graduates from high school with a plan—to date school valedictorian Diane Court (Ione Skye) all summer until she leaves for a fellowship in London. Their love blossoms, even while complicated by future uncertainty and Mr. Court's IRS investigation.

Movie Background Index

STAR WARS (PG) 20th Century Fox, 1977 . . . . 47, 48, 63
Luke Skywalker (Mark Hamill) joins Obi-Wan Kenobi (Alec Guinness), Han Solo (Harrison Ford), and Chewbacca to save Princess Leia (Carrie Fisher) from execution and to destroy the evil Empire's super weapon, the Death Star.

STAR WARS: EPISODE 1–THE PHANTOM MENACE (PG)
20th Century Fox, 1999. . . . . 26, 71, 121
Qui-Gon Jinn (Liam Neeson) and Obi-Wan (Ewan McGregor) help Queen Amidala (Natalie Portman) save her planet from invasion by the Trade Federation. They return to Naboo to fight for freedom, with the help of Jedi prodigy Anakin Skywalker.

STEPMOM (PG-13) Columbia Pictures, 1998. 41
Isabel (Julia Roberts) and Luke (Ed Harris) decide to get married, much to the consternation of Luke's kids Anna and Ben. When his ex-wife, Jackie (Susan Sarandon), finds out she has cancer, Jackie decides to help Isabel learn what it means to be a mother.

THE SURE THING (PG-13) Columbia Pictures, 1985 . . . . 28, 100
Gib (John Cusack) and Alison (Daphne Zuniga) hate each other, but find friendship and love as they make their way across the country for spring break in California.

TITANIC (PG-13) Paramount Pictures, 1997 . . . . 45, 61, 134
Jack (Leonardo DiCaprio) and Rose (Kate Winslet) find star-crossed love on the tragic maiden voyage of the R.M.S. Titanic.

THAT THING YOU DO! (PG) 20th Century Fox, 1996 38
The Wonders hit single "That Thing You Do!" blasts up the charts and forces the band to deal with fame in the '60s and tensions within the band.

THE TRUMAN SHOW (PG) Paramount Pictures, 1998. . . . . . . 51, 75, 119
Truman Burbank (Jim Carrey) is unaware that he lives on a soundstage and is the star of a TV show that broadcasts his life nonstop to the world. Once he begins to see the truth, he struggles to escape into the "real" world.

WAKING NED DEVINE (PG) Fox Searchlight, 1998 68
Ned Devine wins the lottery, and he immediately dies from the shock. Michael and Jackie convince the entire village to pretend that Ned still lives so they can collect the prize money and divide it among themselves.

Index

Movie Background

THE WIZARD OF OZ (G) MGM, 1939 . . . . **32, 59, 102**

Dorothy (Judy Garland) finds herself whisked away from Kansas in a tornado and dumped in the magical land of Oz. She must journey to the great Wizard, with the help of the Tin Woodsman, the Scarecrow, and the Cowardly Lion, to ask for help getting home.

YOU'VE GOT MAIL (PG) Warner Bros., 1998 . . . . **65, 88**

Joe Fox (Tom Hanks) owns the mega-chain bookstore that is driving Kathleen Kelly's (Meg Ryan) small children's bookstore out of business. Their disdain for each other is only matched by the deep love they develop (unknowingly) through an e-mail romance.

Scripture Index

★ ★ ★

Scripture Index

Scripture Index

153

Topical Index

★   ★   ★

Topical Index

Topical Index

use **pop culture** to reach **kids** and **adults** with the **gospel**

The most powerful way to capture the attention of your teenagers and adults is to use gospel-filtered discussion starters drawn from hundreds of popular films, videos, and CDs.

MinistryandMedia.com is a storehouse of pop culture information and programming ideas that will help you use media to relate the gospel to teenagers and adults. Sure, you could sit through 1,000 of hours of videos from the past 40 years or purchase hundreds of CDs of artists from pop to rap to electronic to worship. But who's got the time?

It's already been done by group Magazine's media editor. And it's constantly updated—ready for you to use at **MinistryandMedia.com**:

- Biblical discussion starters using popular films.
- Reviews and gospel tie-ins for classic and new-this-week videos.
- Background information and themes for both Christian and mainstream music releases.
- Reviews of newly released films that many teenagers have seen or plan to see.
- PLUS: Reviews of video games and TV programs.

What do you have planned for this week? Why not start a discussion they'll remember for a lifetime.

MINISTRY and MEDIA.com

recycling pop culture into ministry tools